Shoegaze

Forthcoming in the series:

Shoegaze

Ryan Pinkard

BLOOMSBURY ACADEMIC
NEW YORK • LONDON • OXFORD • NEW DELHI • SYDNEY

BLOOMSBURY ACADEMIC
Bloomsbury Publishing Inc
1385 Broadway, New York, NY 10018, USA
50 Bedford Square, London, WC1B 3DP, UK
29 Earlsfort Terrace, Dublin 2, Ireland

BLOOMSBURY, BLOOMSBURY ACADEMIC and the Diana logo are
trademarks of Bloomsbury Publishing Plc

First published in the United States of America 2024

A catalog record for this book is available from the Library of Congress.

ISBN: PB: 979-8-7651-0341-8
ePDF: 979-8-7651-0343-2
eBook: 979-8-7651-0342-5

Series: Genre: A 33 1/3 Series

Typeset by Deanta Global Publishing Services, Chennai, India

To find out more about our authors and books visit www.bloomsbury.com
and sign up for our newsletters.

Contents

Shoegaze Voices

Greg Ackell – Drop Nineteens

Emma Anderson – Lush

Andy Bell – Ride

Miki Berenyi – Lush

Polly Birkbeck – PR

Laurence "Loz" Colbert – Ride

Nick Chaplin – Slowdive

Nathaniel "Nat" Cramp – Label Head, Sonic Cathedral

Adam Franklin – Swervedriver

Mark Gardener – Ride

Rachel Goswell – Slowdive

Robin Guthrie – Cocteau Twins

Neil Halstead – Slowdive

Jimmy Hartridge – Swervedriver

Sonic Boom (a.k.a. Pete Kember) – Spacemen 3

Paul Lester – Journalist, *Melody Maker*

J Mascis – Dinosaur Jr.

Ian Masters – Pale Saints

Alan McGee – Label Head, Creation Records

K. J. "Moose" McKillop – Moose

Alan Moulder – Producer

Stephen Patman – Chapterhouse

David Quantick – Journalist, *NME*

Steve Queralt – Ride

Chris Roberts – Journalist, *Melody Maker*

Jane Savidge – Author and PR

Christian Savill – Slowdive

Simon Scott – Slowdive

Andy Sherriff – Chapterhouse

Steve Sutherland – Editor, *NME* & *Melody Maker*

Introduction

What the hell is shoegaze? To be honest, I had no idea when I began this book. *Is it a genre? A scene? A movement? A sound?* By various definitions it's any combination of those things. Back in the '90s, many would have said it was entirely fabricated—the term "shoegaze" a bullshit, offensive label given by the notoriously catty and scene-obsessed British music press that was plainly rejected by the absurdly small collection of bands to which it supposedly applied.

Today shoegaze is undeniable. As a descriptor and as a source of influence, it is used in more ways and by more bands than anyone could have imagined thirty years ago. Its very vagueness gives off an aura of cool. Between those periods of invention and ubiquity, the term—along with the bands it first described—all but disappeared off the face of the earth, or at least the radars of British and American music critics.

Let me be the first to tell you: I did not embark on this investigation as the world's most obvious expert on shoegaze. As an American who was literally an infant when the term was coined, I wasn't there on the ground when the original phenomenon occurred, and after discovering it in my teens, I was by no means a shoegaze fanatic. Like any indie kid who read *Pitchfork* in the late Aughts (the Noughties for British readers), I was aware enough of classic albums like Ride's *Nowhere*, Slowdive's *Souvlaki*, and of course My Bloody Valentine's

Loveless to have a fuzzy sense of what constituted this so-called genre in terms of sound and feeling, but I honestly had no clue of what lay beneath the tip of the shoegaze iceberg. I suspect this is most people's position.

This begs the question: *Who am I to write the book on shoegaze?* Well, for one thing, I appear to be the only one curious enough to do so in the more than three decades since it appeared. And to compensate for my lack of firsthand knowledge, I chose to position this book as an oral history that collects the memories and perspectives of thirty musicians, label heads, producers, and journalists who *were* there when shoegaze was born, crucified, and resurrected. Plus, as I learned, this short-lived, distinctly British and Gen X phenomenon is really only being talked about today because of American millennials like me who picked it out of the dustbin and ran with it.

Because shoegaze has never been properly defined, there are a number of ways I could have approached it. If you were hoping for a comprehensive guide to the countless releases that have been described as *shoegaze*, *shoegaze-inspired*, or worst of all, *nu-gaze* over the years, you will be disappointed, though if you're interested in that, *Pitchfork*'s list of "The 50 Best Shoegaze Albums of All Time" is a good place to start. Similarly, for the sake of inclusivity, I could have taken a wide-definition that encompasses the huge number of bands that at some point broached a shoegazey sound, as Cherry Red Records summed up wonderfully with their rich 5CD box set, *Still in a Dream: A Story of Shoegaze 1988–1995*.

Instead, this particular book takes an exceedingly narrow approach, focusing on the first wave of shoegaze: the core bands, their sounds, their influence, and their journeys in and out of obscurity. En route, we'll explore how the terms "shoegaze," "shoegazing," and "The Scene That Celebrates Itself" may or may not have been appropriate descriptions at the time, and how shoegaze evolved into something much larger than it began as. In this way, the book also functions as a case study of *genre* itself and its various qualities and shortcomings.

While I was as skeptical as anyone going into it, I became fascinated by shoegaze and the unlikely odyssey of this esoteric, experimental music form, which nearly became a mainstream entity (at least in the UK), only to be viciously killed off, forgotten, and rediscovered by a new generation that regards it as one of the most influential alternative music events since the Velvet Underground.

1 What Is Shoegaze?

Throughout this book, shoegaze will be imprecisely referred to—by me and the many people I interviewed—as a genre, a scene, a sound, even a philosophy. At the same time, I will put forth this working definition of shoegaze for the sake of scope and argument:

> **Shoegaze** (*noun, shoe·gaze, "'shü-ˌgāz"*), also referred to as **shoegazing**, is a style of music that first emerged in Southern England in the late '80s. Typically identified by its noisy, effects-laden guitar, obfuscated vocals, and atmospheric production, it was principally inspired by bands like Cocteau Twins, the Jesus and Mary Chain, Sonic Youth, Dinosaur Jr, and, above all, My Bloody Valentine. After peaking in the early '90s, the original shoegaze scene—which included core acts Ride, Slowdive, Lush, Chapterhouse, Swervedriver, and Moose—quickly lost popularity and faded into history, only to be rediscovered and gain an outsized influence in the new millennium where it continues to inspire new generations of musicians and fans.

So then, according to the people who make it, what does shoegaze sound like?

Steve Queralt (Ride): If you're in a band of four people—two guitarists, a bass, and a drummer—it's quite an easy sound to make.

Nick Chaplin (Slowdive): It's primarily loud guitar music with vocals sunk in the mix.

Andy Bell (Ride): The most conspicuous effects are reverb, an ethereal vocal style, and an atmospheric sound. It has a kind of drugginess or narcotic feeling. There's definitely an otherworldliness to this misty, foggy sound.

Nathaniel Cramp (Sonic Cathedral): It's slightly out-of-focus and blurry, due to the distortion, delay, and reverb. It's got a weird melancholic euphoria that's both happy and sad. It's almost a feeling more than a sound.

Andy Sherriff (Chapterhouse): It's romantic and generally quite intelligent, but there's also moments of exhilaration, where you have sweeping pure pop energy hidden in this beautiful textured noise.

Rachel Goswell (Slowdive): For me, shoegaze is about the washes of sounds and the emotions that it evokes in you, which can be quite fierce.

Simon Scott (Slowdive): There are some really good pop melodies, and there's some really filthy, nasty noise. Nothing's quite definitive, and as a listener, you can get inside the song and almost reflect it back on something that's happening in your life, so there's a real emotional resonance. It kind of opens a window into your daydreams.

Jane Savidge (PR): The sound is so all-encompassing and wonderfully warming. It makes you fly off into space mentally in a way that very few sounds can do. In a lot of ways, it's got more in common with techno than rock music because it really flips your mind.

Despite their common ground, one of the first things most original shoegazers will tell you is that the bands don't actually sound that much alike.

Emma Anderson (Lush): We started getting lumped in with bands like Ride, Slowdive, Moose, and Chapterhouse, even though I'm not even sure the music is that similar. A lot of it was press-created. They were very into labels and categorizing and putting people in little pigeon holes.

Adam Franklin (Swervedriver): When you go to Spotify, it puts Swervedriver and Lush together under "Similar Artists." I think Swervedriver sounds more like Dinosaur Jr. than Lush, but that's a different genre as far as what Wikipedia tells us.

Neil Halstead (Slowdive): The influences were all coming from a similar place, and there was a willingness to explore the sonic palette in a way that wasn't happening with mainstream music, or even indie music.

Stephen Patman (Chapterhouse): The only thing the bands really shared was coming from a similar period in time and being influenced by similar input, but what each band went and did with that was incredibly diverse.

While there are various definitions and approaches allowed under the shoegaze umbrella, in recent years, one band's sound has become most synonymous with the shoegaze sound.

Andy Sherriff: I suppose the only pure shoegaze band is Slowdive. Everyone else is either a bit more rocky, or a bit more dancey, or a bit more pop. If you do a shoegaze litmus test, they would be the archetype to base everything on.

Stephen Patman: Slowdive really became the unadulterated essence of shoegaze. I think that's why they've become the poster boys for the whole scene, because it doesn't deviate in any way from this very specific sound that's almost a distillation of what shoegaze is.

J Mascis (Dinosaur Jr.): I know Kevin [Shields of My Bloody Valentine] said he thought that Slowdive was the poster child of shoegaze. Like, if you look up "shoegaze" in the dictionary, Slowdive would be the definition.

Now if shoegaze has one basic formula, it is based upon a particular combination of noise and melody that creates a dreamy, psychedelic atmosphere for the listener. While you could lose another common trait—such as soft, buried vocals—and still potentially squeeze it into the shoegaze category, it simply isn't shoegaze without the sonic aura created by juxtaposing a discernible tune with a certain degree of fuzz, distortion, or reverb.

Loz Colbert (Ride): In the '60s and '70s, and even more so in the '80s, noise was a bad thing—something that people tried to get rid of.

Mark Gardener (Ride): When you've got dark and heavy noise against beautiful melodies and harmonies, that contrast just sounds amazing.

When heard in a live setting, this beautiful noise is also played at incredible, ear-bleeding volumes.

J Mascis: At certain volumes you can definitely hear different things. I remember seeing Motörhead when I was a kid and feeling like I could lean back and the sound would hold me up. I'm just chasing that feeling of being enveloped in sound.

Neil Halstead: It needs to surround you. If it's too quiet, it becomes underwhelming.

Nick Chaplin: We *have* to be loud. When you get to a certain volume, you start to invent sounds in your head as a listener. In conjunction with the physical aspect of it, where you can feel it vibrating in your body, we always wanted to pursue that.

Chris Roberts (*Melody Maker*): These bands would be ridiculously loud. You'd go to a tiny club, and it'd be rammed. The noise would be bouncing off the walls, and you'd be swamped and enveloped by it. It was way too loud, but it was part of the experience. You *wanted* it to be euphorically excessive, so that when you came away from a Ride or a Chapterhouse gig, you'd say, *Now that was a gig!*

Mark Gardener: Subjecting people to that kind of noise made an impact in rooms in a very obvious way. We'd go in and just turn our amps really loud. In the smaller venues the soundman would point out that our amps were louder than the PA, so people were not hearing our vocals at all, but of course we were like, *That's how we wanna sound*. In a weird way, it worked for us. That chaos was part of why it was great.

The way these all-important noises are achieved is predominantly through guitar pedals and effects processors, which have the ability to take an instrument's basic soundwave and modify it in unique and interesting ways. Like mad scientists, shoegazers would experiment relentlessly, often combining multiple effects in search of never-before-heard sounds. The operation of these effects via intricate circuits of foot-activated pedal boards—which necessitates the guitarist to frequently look down at their feet—is at least one explanation for the name "shoegaze."

Sonic Boom (Spacemen 3): Kevin [Shields] was the first person I ever saw who had a pedal board. In Spacemen 3 we only had one pedal each.

J Mascis: When I was learning guitar, there were a lot of older guitar purists who only wanted to plug right into an amp, but I always had pedals from the start. It's like there was a whole new generation of guitarists who were playing pedals as part of their guitar.

Miki Berenyi (Lush): I do think a lot of that experimentation with pedals had to do with the fact that pedals were suddenly quite cheap and you could get a lot of them secondhand.

Alan Moulder (Producer): It was pedal mania. There were new ones coming out all the time. You had the reverb pedals, which can give that blurry effect that sounds more like a string section, and delays, which feed into each other to create this massive ocean of sound. With all these bands there was time and willingness to experiment. It'd be like going into the laboratory.

Jimmy Hartridge (Swervedriver): You change the dynamics instantly by pressing on a pedal. When you don't have to stick with one tone, why would you? There are so many new colors you can play with. The potential is so great.

Nick Chaplin: We always joke about what we would do if we didn't have the pedal boards, because sometimes on tour you get off a flight and you're waiting for your luggage to come around that conveyor belt, and it's like, *Where are the pedal boards?!* You can pick up any guitar and play it. Drums are drums. But the pedals are so crucial to the sound that we make, we couldn't do the show without them. They give the band its sound.

Being that shoegaze is all about experimental guitar that's pushed to the foreground, the vocals are correspondingly pushed to the background of the mix, often to the point where the lyrics themselves are indecipherable. While some have said that this dynamic was partly due to the singers' lack of confidence, the resulting sound, which adds to the dreamy atmospheres while acting as a delicate contrast to the abrasive guitar, became something to which shoegazers aspired.

Alan Moulder: A lot of them were quite shy—which is where "shoegaze" came from—so having their vocals tucked in a little bit, rather than right on top, probably made them feel a bit more comfortable.

Andy Sherriff: There was some strong songwriting in shoegaze, but it was all hidden away because everyone had these vocals that were mixed down low.

Rachel Goswell: The buried vocals are really integral to the shoegaze sound, because it's using the voice more as another instrument rather than it being singled out.

Moose McKillop (Moose): The idea was to have these beautifully constructed vocal harmonies and introspective lyrics, but swamped with guitars that are intruding all over the place.

Robin Guthrie (Cocteau Twins): The difference between working with a shoegaze band and a normal band in the studio is that in a normal band, the singer comes up to the mixing desk and asks you to push the vocals up in the mix, whereas a shoegaze singer asks you to fade it down.

While the buried vocals are an essential and endearing quality among the shoegaze faithful, they became a sticking point for critics and naysayers.

Steve Sutherland (*NME, Melody Maker*): The way most people deal with popular music is via singing along with the lyrics. But with shoegaze they have no lyrics, or at least you can't hear them, so there's no way you can participate except to admire in a weird sort of way. You can get lost in the music, but you can't actually be part of it.

Perhaps unsurprisingly, shoegaze is not an especially visual art form. Music videos were few. Fashion was an afterthought. Live productions were mostly limited to moody lighting. The very name "shoegaze" comes, in part, from the grumbling observation that these bands were press-shy and barely moved while on stage. For listeners this either added an intriguing dimension of mystery to the already enigmatic sounds, or it was a pretentious and boring turnoff. For the musicians, it was a consequence of their predominantly introverted personalities and their prevailing belief that the music should speak for itself. This non-look became a look in itself.

Andy Sherriff: Shoegazing was the opposite of putting your foot on the monitor. There was a practical side to looking down at your guitar and pedals, but it was also a bit of a shield, because we weren't rock gods. There was no attempt to put on a show because that wasn't what we were interested in.

Mark Gardener: We didn't wanna use the stage as a place to go ego-overload and stomp around like the stadium rock bands of the time. It taps into that underground feeling, where you just do the music. You make the racket and you don't have to prance around like a prat.

Miki Berenyi: Sometimes you'd go to a gig and you could barely see the band. It wasn't about putting a spotlight on the lead singer, who's gonna be giving some fucking attitude. It was quite anti-star, which is also why it got a lot of criticism.

Jane Savidge: It's meant to show that you don't want to connect with the audience, and because of that, it connects with the audience. I think that's one of the great things about shoegazing—that disassociation is recognized by the audience as a disassociation. Like a "Death to the Pixies" T-shirt, it's a knowing glance at your followers.

Adam Franklin: I think it became a badge of honor, not really saying stuff to the audience. Like, "We're just gonna plow on. Here's the next song."

Following in the footsteps of My Bloody Valentine, Cocteau Twins, Pixies, and Sonic Youth—but in contrast with the vast majority of scenes preceding it—a notable element to the look and sound of shoegaze was the presence of one or more women in the bands.

Sonic Boom: That was a healthy thing about shoegaze. You started to see girls in bands more, which is a good energy. It was quite unusual at the time. Bands were always a bunch of dudes.

Steve Sutherland: A larger percentage of the musicians in those bands were female than there'd probably ever been before. There was none of that "only boys can play guitar" malarkey, and the sensibility of it was much more sensitive.

Nick Chaplin: We weren't as macho as other bands of the era. A lot of the shoegaze bands had some female influence, even if it sometimes seemed like, *Oh, we need a girl in the band because that's what shoegaze bands have.*

Simon Scott: There's definitely more of a balance of masculine and feminine in shoegaze. You can hear that in the way that you've got Neil and Rachel's vocals mixed together [in Slowdive], or Kevin and Bilinda [in My Bloody Valentine].

Neil Halstead: The bands that influenced us—Sonic Youth, My Bloody Valentine, Cocteau Twins—all had a strong female presence, but it never really crossed our minds. At the time it seemed totally normal to me, but looking back it seems kind of unique.

As pleasantly progressive as it all sounds, it didn't necessarily feel like some futuristic rock utopia to the actual women in these bands.

Rachel Goswell: It's funny, because if I sat down and thought about it, I'd probably go, *Yeah, there were loads of women*, but my interactions with those women were few and far between. Aside from Miki [from Lush], I didn't really meet any of them, so it's hard for me to say it felt like there were a lot of women.

Emma Anderson: You had Rachel in Slowdive, you had two women in My Bloody Valentine, there's Toni Halliday if you count Curve, and the audiences were quite mixed. I'd like to think that we influenced some other girls to pick up guitars, form bands, and write songs especially, but it's not really a subject that I dwell on.

Rachel Goswell: By default, being a female in a band, you get pushed to the front of pictures, which used to really annoy me. I think it irritated Neil to a certain extent too.

Miki Berenyi: To me [shoegaze] was the ideal, with that idea of elbowing in with your identity. Yes, you would get the music press pushing Rachel from Slowdive and Bilinda, like, *Oh, look at these pretty, fey girls*, but it was much more about the music. I would argue that the blokes in the shoegaze movement were allowed to be more themselves too.

Rachel Goswell: I think we all had very different experiences. I know Miki's experiences of misogyny have been much greater than mine. In Lush, she and Emma were very much the focus of that band, and she was very powerful and outspoken. Back then I was quite shy and didn't particularly relish the attention, so I feel like I just blended in with my bandmates and didn't think about being in a band full of blokes.

A final interesting aspect to shoegaze is how many of its most important releases were neither singles nor full-length albums, but rather extended plays, or EPs. Typically released on CD and twelve-inch vinyl for around £3.99—compared to £6.99 or £8.99 for an LP—these EPs might comprise three to five tracks, although the magic number was four.

Adam Franklin: When you're talking about shoegaze, you *have* to think about the EPs. All the bands were releasing them. Ride released their first EP, which is four songs, and that became a thing. Chapterhouse did it. Slowdive did it. We did it.

Jane Savidge: There were no B-sides in shoegaze, and no shoegaze band advertised themselves with one amazing single. Shoegazing was value-for-money four-track EPs. It might have been to do with the fact that record companies weren't signing album deals. They just thought, *We'll sign this band, record four tracks, and see what happens.*

Christian Savill (Slowdive): EPs seemed to come really naturally to us. We were still super young and inexperienced in a studio, so it was a really nice format to experiment with that was less daunting than doing an album.

Ian Masters (Pale Saints): With an EP you get a chance to show different facets of the band without having to worry if it's gonna be a cohesive album.

Andy Sherriff: At the time there were a lot of pop acts putting out extended 45s, so it was the antithesis of that. Four tracks kind of defines you as a band, like a calling card. It makes people go, *Oh yeah, I like this band. I might go and see them.*

Robin Guthrie: A single doesn't tell the story of the artist. It's just a tune. An EP takes you on a journey.

2 Shoegaze Ancestors

One of shoegaze's main legacies is how it pushed guitar-driven rock into fresh new territory and subsequently inspired countless artists in its wake. But before breaking down the trailblazing sound of shoegaze and how it went on to influence others, we should first explore the tradition of psychedelic explorers, anti-stars, and noisemakers from whence it came. Conveniently, one common trait that no one seems to argue with is that the first wave of shoegazers all drew from the same core influences.

By the mid-'80s, perhaps as a counter-reaction to the overpolished pop and rock of the late '70s and early '80s, there was a newfound interest in the music of the '60s. Specifically, there was a rediscovery of the psychedelic pop of the Beatles, the Beach Boys, and the Byrds, the experimental art rock of the Velvet Underground, the jagged proto-punk of the Stooges and the MC5, and the underground garage rock found on the *Nuggets* compilations and the even more obscure *Pebbles* series.

In the United States, these same influences had already sparked the rich, harmonic Paisley Underground sound, typified by LA groups like Rain Parade and the Dream Syndicate. In Northern England it was fused with dance music to birth Madchester and the "Second Summer of Love," as soundtracked by acts like the Stone Roses, Happy Mondays, and the Charlatans. In Southern England these sonic ancestors would give birth to shoegaze.

Simon Scott: In the little town I was from, I would walk around the concrete streets at night, really bored with a bottle of cider, listening to *Psychocandy* or *Sonic Flower Groove* by Primal Scream. Those were the records that made you think, *Where's this coming from?* And then you'd go, *Oh, I need to listen to the Velvet Underground and Nico*. And then Suicide. And then the Stooges. I would say it goes all the way back to the Byrds, Love, and the '60s garage stuff like the 13th Floor Elevators, the Chocolate Watchband, and the *Nuggets* compilations. You hear the real origins of shoegaze in there.

Mark Gardener: Growing up, our dads were into the Beach Boys and the Beatles, so those records were always there as a foundation. I remember my uncle sat me down when I was six or seven and played me the Byrds, and that blew my mind.

Alan Moulder: The influences were very '60s, with the Beach Boys, the Beatles, and the Phil Spector "Wall of Sound." I think we were trying to turn that into something from our era that was more violent, more of a sonic assault.

Moose McKillop: If you listen to Lush or Moose or the Boo Radleys, we tried to bring a bit of the Beach Boys into it. We'd listen to *Pet Sounds* and *Holland* and *Surf's Up* an awful lot, because those albums have a real language of beauty.

Adam Franklin: I feel like the template for shoegaze is probably "Tomorrow Never Knows" by the Beatles. Surely that's the first shoegaze song, with all those samples and weird horn sounds that are being spliced together.

Neil Halstead: Shoegaze would not be shoegaze without the Byrds. It's jangly, perfect pop that's slightly outta this world. It's got the harmonies, and the guitars always come up around the vocals. If you take "Eight Miles High" and get Sonic Youth to play it, that's shoegaze right there.

Adam Franklin: I mean, apart from anything else, half of Ride and Slowdive dressed like the Byrds—with stripy tops, bowl cuts, and Rickenbackers—so the clues were there.

Jumping ahead a decade, the emergence of UK punk in 1976 marked "Year Zero" for alternative music in Britain. And while the Sex Pistols and the Clash were largely irrelevant for shoegazers musically speaking, the revolution they sparked ushered in the DIY ethos, fanzine culture, and indie labels of the '80s.

Shoegaze would be nothing if not for the incredibly rich decade of indie and alternative rock that preceded it. The UK in particular was a hotbed for inventive bands—not to mention influential indie labels like Factory and Rough Trade—including Joy Division/New Order, the Fall, the Smiths, the Cure, Echo and the Bunnymen, and Siouxsie and the Banshees.

Nick Chaplin: A lot of people miss the goth influence on shoegaze bands. It was certainly apparent when I joined Slowdive that Rachel was a huge goth with her blonde Siouxsie Sioux hair.

By the mid- to late '80s, you also had a handful of American bands on British indies—like fuzz-rocking 4AD signees the Pixies and Throwing Muses—as well as the so-called "C86" scene—which included Primal Scream, the Mighty Lemon Drops, the Soup Dragons, and the Pastels—whose eclectic sounds frequently incorporated jangly guitars and power pop melodies.

Popping out of the UK alternative scene with their 1982 debut on 4AD, *Garlands*, Scottish trio the Cocteau Twins had a keystone influence on what became shoegaze. This had much to do with their dreamy, atmospheric sound, masterminded by guitarist-producer Robin Guthrie, as well as the otherworldly singing of Elizabeth Fraser, whose unintelligible and frequently nonsensical vocals were buried cryptically deep in the mix. Just try listening to a song like 1983's "Sugar Hiccup" or 1990's "Cherry-coloured Funk" and deny their influence on the swirling sounds of Slowdive, Chapterhouse, and Lush.

Mark Gardener: Robin Guthrie was probably the godfather of that whole [shoegaze] sound.

Paul Lester (*Melody Maker*): When *Head Over Heels* came out in '83, it was a new kind of noise. I was never a massive fan of guitars, but this was a different kind of radiated sound.

Robin Guthrie: I was just trying to make something that was otherworldly and not just using the guitar as you're supposed to. I don't know how we influenced [the shoegazers], but I certainly used to see lots of them at our concerts, down at the front of the stage, looking at my pedals more than they were looking at the band.

J Mascis: The Cocteau Twins were awesome, but they didn't have the drums of shoegaze. If you put more fuzz into Cocteau Twins and then add Keith Moon, you'd have shoegaze.

If one of shoegaze's defining characteristics is its particular fusion of noise and melody, then the first band you could reasonably accuse of being shoegaze is another seminal Scottish act: the Jesus and Mary Chain. Released on Creation Records in 1984, the band's debut single, "Upside Down," buries a '60s pop melody, big beat drums, and Jim Reid's mumbling vocals under violent screeches resembling amplified nails on a chalkboard.

J Mascis: The Mary Chain were probably the forefathers of shoegaze. They were all about the fuzz, but then they have these melodies like the Beach Boys. It was like good pop music with a whitewash of noise behind it, but they didn't have the same rock element as shoegaze.

Loz Colbert: For me the epiphany came from listening to *Psychocandy*, where I realized noise could be so overwhelming in a sensory and emotional way. It could explain feelings that couldn't be explained through incredible lyrics or artistic guitar playing or virtuosic singing.

Chris Roberts: The Mary Chain's early gigs, before "Just Like Honey" or "April Skies," were just this ear-splitting assault of white noise. It was pretty horrible actually, but you had to be there. It was just feedback, but it was kind of an art statement, and they influenced the shoegaze bands in the sense of, *Oh, you can do that?* Now noise was part of the palette.

Alan McGee (Creation Records): When I went to sign them, I never even knew they had great songs. At first it was just a great noise. It was extreme.

One step behind the Mary Chain and one step ahead of shoegaze were Spacemen 3 and Loop—two fiercely independent and criminally underrated groups from provincial towns in England who released their first albums in 1986 and 1987, respectively. Eschewing all pop sensibilities, these bands revitalized the psychedelic space rock of the '60s—think the Velvet Underground, Hawkwind, or the Beatles' "Flying"—by leaning into droning, heavy, distorted guitar trips that were also openly drug-influenced, none more explicitly than with Spacemen 3's 1990 release, *Taking Drugs to Make Music to Take Drugs To*.

Nick Chaplin: Spacemen 3 and Loop had that super cool kind of Velvet [Underground] vibe, except the noise they made was just astonishing. The volume, the feedback, the repetitive drone of it—it wasn't really like anything else that was going on at the time. We were really impressed with that visceral noise that you got from those bands, which we then tried to incorporate ourselves.

Sonic Boom: Spacemen 3 could be called a shoegaze band by the fact that we did not have any stage moves. We were just a bunch of dysfunctional, fucked up kids who were into repetition, fuzz, wah-wah, and tremolo, trying to create these druggy textures with our music. Me and Jason [Pierce, later of Spiritualized fame] used to sit down on chairs and just look at our guitars on stage. We were always the anti-performers like that. It was all about the sound we were trying to create and not how we were trying to look.

While taking notes from the rich patchwork of alternative bands that blanketed Britain in the mid-'80s, the shoegazers were also looking across the Atlantic to American indie rockers like Sonic Youth, Dinosaur Jr., and Hüsker Dü. Among their other legacies, these bands were highly instructive for their dynamic interplay of noise and melody, and their powerful use of guitar effects, which had an especially strong impact on harder-rocking shoegazers like My Bloody Valentine, Swervedriver, and early Ride.

J Mascis: In England and Europe they would all say, "Oh, you sound so American," or "The way you play guitar is very American." We're so inundated with classic rock on the radio that that's a bigger backbone of an American sound. It's just a more aggressive guitar style. That's the only difference I can see.

Neil Halstead: I loved the dissonant but melodic interplay of the guitars on Sonic Youth records like *Sister*, *Evol*, and *Daydream Nation*. I guess they influenced us with the idea that you didn't need to be in a conventional tuning, that you could just mess around until you got something that sounded cool.

Jimmy Hartridge: We liked the heaviness of Dinosaur Jr., but the great thing about them is that they're very heavy and very melodic at the same time. It's heavy like Black Sabbath, but their melodies are super influenced by the Beatles. A nice melody is like a nursery rhyme. You could play it to your grandmother, and she'd say, "That's a nice melody," but with the music underneath, you can do anything.

Adam Franklin: Hüsker Dü is quite a big band for shoegaze. It's really, really melodic, but with the nastiest sounding guitars you can imagine, and that became the whole template really. It sounds like a simple thing now to marry melody with noise, but it was quite a revelation.

As for shoegaze's contemporaries, the so-called "baggy" bands of the Madchester scene in Northern England represented a separate culture and attitude to what was brewing in the south, despite sharing numerous commonalities and influences.

Paul Lester: There was almost a yin-yang bisection of the alternative music scene. On the one hand, you had this noise pop scene birthed by the Valentines, Dinosaur Jr., Sonic Youth, Hüsker Dü, the Mary Chain, and the Cocteaus. And on the other side, you had what they called "baggy" or "Madchester," which was Happy Mondays, the Stone Roses, the Charlatans, and all that. They were the incalcitrant bad lads of indie-pop, with their baggy music and loudmouth bravado, whereas the shoegazing bands were all shy, looking at their shoes, not talking themselves up in any particular way.

Less remembered and less pigeonholed—though sometimes tossed into the shoegaze category themselves—many people I interviewed have pointed to a handful of bands from the tail end of the '80s that had a similar impact on inspiring the fully realized shoegaze sound. This includes: the House of Love, a Creation Records noise pop group recognized for their harmonies and ornate psychedelic guitar; A. R. Kane, a wildly eclectic duo from East London who released two critically acclaimed albums, *69* and *i*, between 1988 and 1989; Bark Psychosis, an introspective, experimental group who would go on to spark the term "post-rock" with their belated 1994 debut, *Hex*; Kitchens of Distinction, a noisy, Smiths-meets-Echo-and-the-Bunnymen dream pop band frequently reduced by the UK press as a "gay band" for their singer's open sexuality; and the Telescopes, psychedelic space rockers in the vein of Spacemen 3 and Loop.

*

Of course, in the world of shoegaze, one band looms large over the rest. By any modern definition, My Bloody Valentine is the apotheosis of shoegaze. They were the band that minted the sound with their 1988 album, *Isn't Anything*, and the band that forged the genre's most supreme document, 1991's *Loveless*. Yet at the time, they were not part of the shoegaze scene so much as the progenitors of it.

Nick Chaplin: My Bloody Valentine was sort of the blueprint for it. They were on a pedestal, away from everybody else really. We were all trying to play catch up, and in some ways we still are.

Nathaniel Cramp: When I first started reading the music press, they already talked about My Bloody Valentine in a slightly reverential way. They just existed on a different plane. They certainly weren't criticized in the way the other bands were. MBV had already proved themselves in some way.

Moose McKillop: My Bloody Valentine weren't even considered a shoegaze band at the time. They were just My Bloody Valentine, unique and on their own. It was later on when people looked back at that period and started making connections between them, the Cocteau Twins, and the Jesus and Mary Chain on this shoegaze family tree.

Stephen Patman: I think I underplay their influence sometimes because the first thing people mention when they talk about shoegaze is My Bloody Valentine. There's this concept that they were the incubator of all these bands, when in reality it was kind of a parallel existence. They broke some ground just a little ahead of us, but their sound is so very specific, and once we started being in a band, our eyes kind of narrowed down to what we were doing.

But prior to becoming the sacrosanct sultans of shoegaze who could do no wrong in the eyes of critics or fellow shoegazers, MBV was just another indie band from the '80s. First formed in 1983 Dublin, Ireland, by guitarist Kevin Shields, drummer Colm Ó Cíosóig, and vocalist David Conway, the group went through multiple awkward evolutions and lineup changes before morphing into the indie rock gods they are today.

After briefly relocating to the Netherlands and then Germany, the group settled in London in 1985, where they recruited bassist Debbie Googe and released their debut EP, *Geek!* At this stage the band sounded something like a knockoff of the Jesus and Mary Chain, with Conway's gothy vocals recalling the psychobilly of the Cramps. On their next EPs, 1986's *The New Record by My Bloody Valentine* and 1987's

Sunny Sundae Smile, the band had shape-shifted into a jangly, albeit noisy, indie-pop unit linked to the C86 scene.

Paul Lester: They were a bit of a joke circa '86 or '87. They were just another one of those shambling C86 bands that weren't special in any way.

When Conway subsequently quit My Bloody Valentine, the band made a radical decision: rather than replace their lead singer and continue on their course, they added a second guitarist, Bilinda Butcher, who assumed co-singing duties opposite Kevin Shields. With neither vocalist skilled nor confident on a microphone, their childlike harmonizing began to set them apart on their next releases, the twelve-inch single "Strawberry Wine" and the mini-album *Ecstasy*, which took them one step closer to shoegaze.

Paul Lester: If you listened to "Strawberry Wine" afterward, you realized that they were grappling toward something, but nobody could have predicted what they would become.

By 1988, the final piece of the puzzle fell into place when Kevin Shields stumbled upon a new approach to guitar playing. Specifically inspired by a song called "Apartment 6" by American psych-rockers Green on Red, Shields utilized elements like tremolo, reverb, and unusual tunings to create a woozy effect that almost sounds like it's being played in reverse. He called it "glide guitar." The first tune they unleashed at their live shows was "You Made Me Realise," a song of blaring punkish noise and clanging rhythms, held together by the melodic glue of Kevin and Belinda's static-laced harmonies.

Sonic Boom: When we saw them first perform "You Made Me Realise," I was like, *What the fuck just happened with these guys?* I remember going up to Kevin and saying, "Who wrote that fucking song, dude? Is that a cover?" He went, "No, it's a new song I've just written." I was like, "Jesus Christ, man . . . *Really* nice."

Neil Halstead: They suddenly went from being this blissed-out, super trebly indie band to sounding like the Byrds crossed with Sonic Youth.

It was only then that the band caught the interest of Creation Records head Alan McGee.

Alan McGee: I knew them in 1985 or 1986, when they were kind of like a noisy version of the Pastels. Then I saw them in January '88, and they'd morphed into the Irish Hüsker Dü or something. It was brilliant and I signed them.

While the band already had devotees, it was their debut release on Creation where the shoegaze sound was first fully, shall we say, *realized* on record. Crashing into earth on August 8, 1988, their five-song EP, *You Made Me Realise*, sent shockwaves through the future shoegaze scene.

Paul Lester: The big bang of it all was My Bloody Valentine's *You Made Me Realise* EP. That was just massive, incredible, like the explosion of a sun. It was a new culmination of this noise aesthetic. Robin Guthrie's production had inspired all sorts of critical verbosity, like "sonic cathedrals" and "towering spires of sound," but what Kevin Shields did on *You Made Me Realise* was a level above that.

Moose McKillop: At the time it was revolutionary. It was like, *Wow, why hasn't anybody ever done guitars like that before?* It was absolutely amazing.

Simon Scott: They became this incredibly influential band for everybody—Chapterhouse, Ride, obviously us [in Slowdive]. MBV was everybody's favorite band.

That same autumn, they tripled down on this revelatory new sound, first with the *Feed Me with Your Kiss* EP in October and then their debut full-length, *Isn't Anything*, in November. Ranking the LP number 3 in their Albums of the Year list, *Melody Maker* wrote, "*Isn't Anything* is raving nymphomania and out-of-body experience," while describing how their "langorous [sic] vocals and out-of-focus guitars" slip the listener to the "brink of unconsciousness" like a narcotic, before concluding that the album "establishes them as absent-minded rulers of this daydream nation."[1]

Paul Lester: *Isn't Anything* is the *Sgt. Pepper* of shoegazing. You could just hear everyone's ears prick up. It was a Sex Pistols moment, where 10,000 teenagers around the country decided to form a band in the wake of My Bloody Valentine. And so, before long, a whole scene had been created.

Christian Savill: I'd go and see My Bloody Valentine play live and study what Kevin was playing on guitar and memorize it. Then I'd come home and try to play what he'd played, and it sounded like shit. When Stephen from Chapterhouse pointed out he tunes his guitar in these weird drone tunings, it opened up an entirely new world for a young Slowdive. It added a completely different dimension.

Paul Lester: There were really brilliant writers like Simon Reynolds who were inventing all sorts of new vocabulary to deal with this incredible new sound. They basically attributed Kevin Shields, alongside Sonic Youth and Hüsker Dü, with the "reinvention of the rock guitar." It wasn't cock rock—it was a whole new way of holding and playing the guitar, of new tones and textures. It was rock guitar reborn.

Chris Roberts: The reviews of that time are just so over the top, my own included. It really knocked everyone sideways. *This* was the kind of music we wanted—something challenging, new, and refreshing, and yet it had melodies. It was this mashup of quite sweet tunes and sonic assaults, and it rocked our worlds. Kevin Shields quickly became this enigmatic character, which really wasn't his own doing. He was just a quiet, averagely shy guy, but it led to him being painted as this reclusive genius.

Alan McGee: I was as obsessed with My Bloody Valentine as anybody else. I signed My Bloody Valentine, and then I signed Slowdive, Moonshake, Adorable, the Boo Radleys, the Telescopes, Swervedriver, Ride . . . All these bands were probably signed off the back of me signing the Valentines and trying to go down some weird path that they had opened up.

3 Shoegaze Origins

According to the popular narrative, My Bloody Valentine dropped *You Made Me Realise*, and the rest of the shoegaze flock formed the next day. In truth, it was a bit more gradual than that, with half the groups coming together before the genre's supposed inception date.

With its dueling female songwriters—Emma Anderson and Miki Berenyi—Lush was one of shoegaze's most commercially successful acts, not to mention the earliest to form. Like many of the other bands to follow, the group was started by school-age friends whose first connection dates back to the early '80s.

Miki Berenyi: Me and Emma went to school together when we were about fourteen. We were in a group of girls that started going to see bands. It was a thriving time for cheap gigs, and there were a lot of them every night.

Emma Anderson: Because we were in London, live music was very accessible to us as teenagers. We were quite into goth music, which included the Cocteau Twins. Miki got into that '60s garage rock scene, and I went more into the C86 scene.

Miki Berenyi: There was high unemployment and people had loads of time, so everyone seemed to be in a band, or they were putting out fanzines, or starting up club nights, or designing T-shirts.

After collaborating on a humorous fanzine called *Alphabet Soup*, the girls joined their first bands in 1986, despite barely knowing how to play an instrument.

Miki Berenyi: Emma joined a band called the Rover Girls, and I joined a band called the Bugs, both playing bass. Then, funnily enough, Emma started going out with Kevin Shields, just at the time when My Bloody Valentine were transitioning from being a garage band with Dave as the singer to Bilinda joining.

Emma Anderson: He showed me some chords and basslines, which I found very interesting. I'm not a trained musician, and neither is Kevin, so it was more of an instinctive way of writing music, where you play something and think, *Well this sounds good.* I probably absorbed some of the way he saw chords and melody, and obviously effects and recording techniques.

Miki Berenyi: When they split up, I think it slightly sparked Emma's competitive side. She wanted to write songs and have her own group, so we tentatively formed a band.

Emma Anderson: We ended up rehearsing together in my kitchen. We didn't have a direction. We couldn't even play, really. It was very much that post-punk, DIY, *anyone-can-pick-up-a-guitar* attitude.

Miki Berenyi: When we needed to find a drummer, a bass player, and a singer, I just asked three people at my college, and that's how we ended up with the initial five of us, with Chris Acland, Steve Rippon, and Meriel [Barham] singing.

The band briefly called themselves Baby Machines after a line in a Siouxsie and the Banshees song, before changing their name to Lush, a cool, one-word moniker that would become typical of other shoegaze bands. An early profile of the band written by Chris Roberts would begin, "Lush are nearly as good as their name, which is high praise indeed."[1] Not that they knew what they were doing.

Emma Anderson: There was no master plan. I just started writing songs influenced by what I was into: the Cocteau Twins, the House of Love, My Bloody Valentine. Miki's songs tended to be a bit more jagged and influenced by the Banshees, the garage scene, and the Pixies.

Miki Berenyi: We played a few gigs, and then Meriel seemed to lose interest and left, so we didn't have a singer. Since I was doing backing vocals, I was told that I had to do it, and I was very reluctant. Then, literally the second gig we played, we got reviewed in a huge fucking piece in the *Melody Maker*, so it was like, *Well, you're gonna have to stay the singer now.*

Chris Roberts: I did the first Lush live review, as far as I know. My recollection is that it was pretty good, with strong potential. Miki was kind of a reluctant singer at first. As quaint as it sounds, it was positive to see two women in a band at that time.

Robin Guthrie: At first they were nonsense live, but they became one of the best live bands through touring and growing up in public.

Emma Anderson: As time went on, I thought, *We've got something here*, and it was worth sending a demo out to record labels. So I did.

Through Kevin Shields, Emma took a job with Jeff Barrett—the future founder of Heavenly Records, who at the time did press for both Creation and Factory Records—which granted her a great knowledge for navigating the music industry. It's also how the band was introduced to the Cocteau Twins' Robin Guthrie.

Robin Guthrie: The first time I heard them was on a little cassette. It was the "Etheriel" demo and it sounded terrible. You couldn't even hear the voices, but it was noisy, it had attitude, there was fantastic energy, and there was something really interesting in the songwriting.

Despite an offer from Rough Trade's Geoff Travis to release their demo as a single, Travis encouraged Emma to send their tape to fellow London indie 4AD, who he thought would be a better fit given their resemblance to 4AD bands like Cocteau Twins and Throwing Muses.

Emma Anderson: I came home one day to a message on my answerphone going, "Hello, this is Ivo Watts-Russell from 4AD. I like the tape, but there's somebody that works here who's seen you play live and says you're terrible."

Miki Berenyi: Ivo had a plugger called Howard Gough, who ironically left 4AD later to become our manager. He was like, "You can't sign this band, because they're literally the worst band I've ever seen in my life." So Ivo put us in a studio with [producer] John Fryer to convince the rest of the team that, *Okay, they're not great live, but I can hear something in their songs, so let's develop that.*

Around the same 1987 time frame that Lush was coming together in London, their future labelmates were taking shape far to the north in Leeds. Although Pale Saints would have the least interaction with other members of the scene due to their geographic separation, their heavenly sound, timing, and label association made them undeniably shoegaze to most critics and fans.

Growing up in London with a sponge-like curiosity for all forms of music, young Ian Masters was desperate to form a band ever since seeing his first gig—Blondie at the Hammersmith Odeon—when he was sixteen. He would invite schoolmates to his parents' house to drink beer and play music together, but the collaborations never went anywhere, a trend that continued when he moved north to attend college in Birmingham.

Ian Masters: By the time I moved to Leeds, I was about twenty-one or twenty-two, and still hadn't had a proper band. It was April 1987 when I wrote an ad on a postcard and pinned it up on the wall of a local record shop. I mentioned some bands—John Berry, Debussy, the Misunderstood—just making it as eclectic as I could to maximize the number of people who might answer. In true punk fashion I said, "It doesn't matter what you play or how well you play it," because I was convinced that enthusiasm was the most important ingredient.

His prayers were finally answered when guitarist Graeme Naysmith and drummer Chris Cooper reached out.

Ian Masters: I turned up to the first meeting with an autoharp. I had no idea what kind of music Graeme and Chris made, so

I just thought I'd take something portable—and maybe we'd have a jam with a violin, a tuba, and an autoharp—but it was fairly obvious as soon as we started talking that they wanted to make rock music, so I had to go out and buy a bass guitar, which I'd never played until then.

Despite their direction being somewhat incidental, the founding trio wasted no time venturing into the noisier territories of rock being explored by bands of the day, with few constraints for how loud and nasty they could sound.

Ian Masters: We used to rehearse on a farm in the countryside outside Leeds. The only other inhabitants were cows, so we could just crank it up as far as the amps would go, with total freedom to make as much noise as we wanted.

Gigging around various Leeds pubs, the group started homing in on a sound that balanced noisy atmospheres, retro pop melodies, and Ian's delicate falsetto, often filling in gaps between their songs with loops of incidental music. By the latter half of 1988, after recording some primitive demos on their own four-track equipment, they began seeking a studio that could help them capture what they heard in their heads, eventually meeting a Leeds deejay called Mike Stout and his partner Richard Formby.

Ian Masters: They both had encyclopedic knowledge of music, especially psychedelic music, and they knew exactly what we wanted. So it was when we got to record with those two sympathetic guys that we started to sound like Pale Saints and felt confident enough to send those tape demos out to a few labels.

When 4AD's Ivo Watts-Russell got in touch, Ian couldn't quite believe it.

Ian Masters: He rang up my house in Leeds after hearing our demo, and I naturally presumed it was one of our mates having a laugh, so the first words I ever said to Ivo were "Fuck off!"

*

One theme that helped the press justify grouping the shoegaze bands together was the fact that many of them came from the Thames Valley, a region immediately west of London that includes the towns of Oxford—home of Ride and Swervedriver—and Reading—birthplace of Chapterhouse and Slowdive.

Simon Scott: It was way broader than that—you had the Pale Saints up in Leeds, I was initially in the Charlottes up in Cambridge, there was Bleach, who were from out east in Ipswich—but there was obviously something in the water, because Oxford and Reading are really close to each other, and Chapterhouse, Slowdive, Swervedriver, and Ride all came out of that area at the same time.

What made these towns a hotbed for shoegaze is a matter of speculation, but they were both university towns an hour or so outside of London that attracted touring indie bands. And although Oxford has since produced a respectable list of rock bands—Radiohead, Supergrass, Foals, Glass Animals—it was not seen as a musical hub in the '80s.

Adam Franklin: There wasn't really a music scene in Oxford. It really wasn't until Ride in 1990 that any Oxford band had a hit record on the charts.

While Swervedriver—the shoegaze scene's most muscular band—wouldn't technically form until 1989, founding members (and only constants) Adam Franklin and Jimmy Hartridge grew up in the nearby village of Wheatley and were active in Oxford going back to the early to mid-'80s, where they quickly filled a void in the city's small musical landscape.

Adam Franklin: In the mid-'80s, there were a lot of bands doing a sort of jangly pop that was nice and melodic, but a bit wimpy. And then there were noisier bands doing more distorted stuff that wasn't melodic enough.

Jimmy Hartridge: I was in a band called the Road Runners with my brother and Adam's brother, and we were much more traditional rock and roll, covering Bo Diddley and the Rolling Stones. Adam was in a band called the Stranded, and they were much more into contemporary gothic stuff, like Echo and the Bunnymen.

Adam Franklin: We all had a similar path, growing up listening to T. Rex, the Sweet, Slade, and then punk. We had a love of '60s psychedelia and the *Pebbles* bands. Then we discovered the Stooges and the MC5, which became the two bands we really latched onto.

Jimmy Hartridge: We all became disenchanted with our other bands, so Adam and I, plus his brother Graham and our friend Paddy, set up a band called Shake Appeal, named after the Stooges song.

With Adam's brother singing lead, future Swervedriver member Adi Vines playing bass, and Paddy Pulzer on drums, Shake

Appeal was quickly recognized as one of the hottest local acts in town—even playing an early London show with a still garage-phase My Bloody Valentine—and voted the best band in Oxford in 1985. Their hard-edged sound left an impression on the soon-to-be members of Ride.

Mark Gardener: I went to an early Shake Appeal show in this small, rough indie venue called the Co-Op Hall. Everybody was smoking pot, and I remember being stoned and watching Shake Appeal, thinking, *Wow, these local guys hit really hard.*

Jimmy Hartridge: We basically did a Stooges rip-off until '88 or '89, at which point we realized that it wasn't really gonna have any impact, because we're basically just rehashing something that had already been done.

Just as Shake Appeal was running out of steam in 1988, the future teenage heartthrobs of Ride—Andy Bell, Mark Gardener, Steve Queralt, and Laurence "Loz" Colbert—were beginning their unmatched ascent to shoegaze's biggest hitmakers.

Andy Bell: The band came out of the Cheney School, which Mark and I both attended from the age of thirteen to seventeen. We became mates through getting into the Smiths and the Cure, and started playing guitar together. Steve was a year or two above us, but we were mates with his brother.

Mark Gardener: As me and Andy were gravitating toward each other, we had a bit of a moment when we were both doing a stage production of *Grease*, of all things, which was the first time that I sang out loud to a lot of people. I was playing the character Doody, so I had to open the show with "Grease is the Word," and Andy was the rock and roll guitar player. I think we both recognized how the other was able to deliver under a pressure situation in front of an audience.

It wasn't until Andy and Mark enrolled in art school in nearby Banbury that they properly connected with Steve, who played bass and worked at a record store, and then met Loz, who completed the four-piece.

Andy Bell: Loz had the drum kit and was sort of the catalyst for us getting together.

Mark Gardener: Our first proper rehearsal was in Loz's mum's garage, in this quiet village in Oxfordshire, and it was a real racket. His mom received quite a lot of complaints for that, but it felt really good.

Steve Queralt: We had no ambitions other than just to get in a garage and make music together, basically playing other people's songs. We tried to do versions of "How Soon Is Now" by the Smiths and "Blue Monday" by New Order.

The foursome decided to call themselves Ride, referencing both their Jack Kerouac-inspired love of motion and the ride cymbal in a drum kit. Despite their penchant for well-crafted '60s pop, their early sound was as loud and abrasive as any of their counterparts.

Mark Gardener: By the time we started to make demos, we definitely knew that we wanted to make an impact. Steve had introduced us to noisy bands like My Bloody Valentine, Cocteau

Twins, and Loop, while Andy and I both loved the Beatles, Byrds, and Beach Boys, so we kind of combined the two.

Andy Bell: We were lucky that we were good at doing what was perfectly suitable for the scene that we became part of. We weren't strong singers—me and Mark had softer voices—so we did a lot of harmonies and made it into a strength. We liked loud guitars with lots of pedals, along with the exciting drums and melodic bass playing, and it all worked really well.

Steve Queralt: Very soon we got our first gig at the art college, and our next ambition was to play the biggest venue in Oxford.

Adam Franklin: I was there at the first [proper] Ride show. I remember being at the soundcheck and thinking, *This band sounds pretty good!* They looked like a bunch of teenagers that were the perfect cross between the Stooges and the Byrds. It was just this fantastic noise coming out.

After that first show, one of the band's early demo tapes—featuring versions of "Chelsea Girl," "Drive Blind," and a song called "I'm Fine Thanks"—got sent to Warner Bros. Records, where Jim Reid of the Jesus and Mary Chain supposedly heard it and approved. Despite having their hearts set on signing to 4AD, the band was wined and dined on the Warner dime—not to mention given £5,000 to record more demos—with the intention that they would sign to a new Warner offshoot created just for them called One Big Guitar.[2] That is, until Alan McGee caught wind of the pending deal.

Alan McGee: I had a meeting at Warner Bros. Records and the A&R guy foolishly played me this band called Ride and said, "I'm having problems with the contract, but I intend to sign them." I thought it was fucking great, so I got out of the meeting and, with one of these early cellular phones I'd just been given in 1989, I phoned my office and said, "Get me the number for Ride." I met the band, followed them around for three or four shows, and then I signed them.

Steve Queralt: It was a no-brainer. I mean, Creation Records had signed all sorts of bands that we were into, so when they offered to put our EP out, we jumped at the chance. That was really the start of everything for us. It happened very, very fast after that.

With Shake Appeal effectively broken up, Adam Franklin wrote a handful of songs for himself that would chart a new course for his bandmates' next evolution: Swervedriver.

Adam Franklin: I didn't have a band, but I wrote three songs and recorded demos, one of which was "Son of Mustang Ford." The song has this American wanderlust, sort of inspired by T. Rex's songs about American cars, which were, of course, based on Chuck Berry's songs about cars. [Bassist] Adi still lived in the same house as me, so when he heard it coming through the floorboards, he said, "Is that you? Right, we're getting the band back together. And you're the singer now."

Jimmy Hartridge: After Adam's brother left the band, we thought we'd contemporize a bit and take it a little bit more seriously. We moved to London in '89 and rehearsed a lot.

Adam Franklin: It was kind of an open secret in Oxford that Ride had been signed to Creation Records. It made us think, *Oh shit, we need to get our skates on!* We made a demo and sent it to a few labels, the first being Blast First because it was the label that licensed Sonic Youth, Dinosaur Jr., and Butthole Surfers in England. At the end we had one tape left over, and we thought, *Let's give it to Mark. He could give it to Alan McGee at Creation.*

Mark Gardener: I gave their demo tape to Alan McGee and said, "I always loved this band when they were Shake Appeal, and now they're Swervedriver. See what you think."

Alan McGee: Mark played me Swervedriver, and I loved it. I *really* loved that band. I'm not sure they were shoegaze. To me they were just rock and roll.

Adam Franklin: We didn't think that they would wanna sign us, but as it turned out, McGee was the first guy to get back in touch. We already knew the people from My Bloody Valentine and Ride, so Creation seemed like the perfect label to sign to.

*

Just a half-hour's drive from Oxford, Chapterhouse and Slowdive had a similarly intertwined origin story in Reading, which was an even less likely place for innovative indie rock to spring up from.

Nick Chaplin: Reading's not a city like Oxford—it's a reasonably sized town. Historically, you associate alternative bands with coming from more edgy environments, but for whatever reason in the late '80s there was us and there was

Chapterhouse, and later Revolver came along from just down the road in Farnham. It was a good testing ground for a lot of these bands before they went off and played shows in London.

Rachel Goswell: There was a little nightclub called the After Dark Club, which I probably frequented seven nights a week in the early days of Slowdive.

Neil Halstead: All the bands we were into at sixteen were playing at this club: Dinosaur Jr., My Bloody Valentine, Spacemen 3, Loop, the House of Love, Teenage Fanclub . . . There was quite a tight scene of indie kids, goths, and alternative types.

Andy Sherriff: There was a scene in the sense that we would all go to Reading from fourteen or fifteen years old and hang out with people that were of a similar persuasion. At the time you were either alternative or you were "casual."

Stephen Patman: There was a culture then called "casuals," which was influenced by the end of the new romantics, but mixed with football hooligans. They'd have Duran Duran haircuts and Pringle jumpers, but then they would beat people up for being weird, like, "Get your fucking hair cut! You're a fucking queer!" If you were alternative in Reading, there were only twenty or thirty people you could hang out with, so it focused all the punks, skinheads, goths, and hippies who weren't into Dire Straits and Live Aid bands in one place.

The elder of the two big Reading bands, Chapterhouse formed in 1987 around childhood friends and singer-guitarists Andrew

Sherriff and Stephen Patman, in addition to third guitarist Simon Rowe, drummer Ashley Bates, and bassist Jon Curtis—that last of whom would be replaced with Russell Barrett by the time they started releasing records.

Stephen Patman: Andy, Simon, and myself grew up in the same suburb of Reading and went to the same secondary school. When Andy moved away, Simon and I got to know each other better and started learning guitar. The summer after we graduated I bumped into Andy in a video store, and we realized we had the same record collections and were all playing guitar, so we all went, *Whoa!*

While Chapterhouse would come to be known for their swirling compositions that are at times delicate and dance-influenced, their foundation was in hard, fast acid rock that could make your head spin. Just like the Doors, the band's name was lifted from Aldous Huxley's *The Doors of Perception*, in which the psychedelic philosopher describes how the architecture of a particular cathedral chamber, or "chapter house," was so ornate that it induced the feeling of tripping on LSD.

Andy Sherriff: It happened quite organically. We just booked a rehearsal room and started covering the Beatles, Byrds, Stooges, Velvet Underground. Then someone came in and said, "Do you wanna play a gig at the pub around the corner?" We were like, "Oh, okay."

Shortly thereafter, with only a handful of gigs under their belts, the young psych-rockers got taken under the wings of two of their heroes: Sonic Boom and J. Spaceman in Spacemen 3.

Stephen Patman: We noticed that Spacemen 3 were coming to the After Dark Club, and I asked the promoter if we could support them, which turned out to be our fourth gig ever. We got chatting backstage, and they were like, "Wow, we really like your stuff."

Sonic Boom: When I first met Chapterhouse, before they became the Chapterhouse that we know, they were a Stooges kind of band. They were *really* good, I have to say.

Stephen Patman: Not long after that, Sonic Boom was interviewed by the press and he named us as his favorite new band. Then he mentioned us to their manager, who got in touch and asked us to do a few shows with them.

Sonic Boom: We played with them a bunch, and I was gonna put out their first record on the label I was starting. It was gonna be an EP with an awesome cover of the Beatles song "Rain" that they used to do.

Stephen Patman: Then their manager started repping us and booked us to record some songs up in the studio they used in Rugby, which formed some of our first few EPs and the first album. From '87 to '90 it was just touring and support slots around London until we got signed by Dedicated Records, who, of course, had just signed Spacemen 3.

The teenage babies of the scene who would become shoegaze's most emblematic act, Slowdive came together a year or so after their friends in Chapterhouse. Once again, their origins trace back even further, when founding vocalists and guitarists Neil Halstead and Rachel Goswell met in primary school.

Rachel Goswell: When we were like fifteen, me and a girl called Allison decided we were gonna start a band. We had our first practice at a Sunday school club that had PA equipment. Neil was the prefect, so he set up the PA and started playing with us. I called Allison the following week, and she was like, "I don't wanna be in a band anymore," so I went back on my own. Neil had set everything up, and there were other kids in our year, so those of us that could play an instrument just congregated around the PA and made noise.

Also present was Adrian Sell, the first of numerous Slowdive drummers, who then brought bassist Nick Chaplin into the fold to form their original four-piece. Initially, the band gave themselves the queasy name "the Pumpkin Fairies."

Neil Halstead: We sounded a bit Sonic Youthy, doing T. Rex covers, a cover of "Rain" by the Cult, and a good version of "Stephanie Says." When we started writing our own songs, we decided we needed another guitarist, and we thought it would be nice to have another girl in the band to kinda balance it out.

Christian Savill: There was this local little fanzine where they placed a small ad for a guitarist, and I thought, *Shall I reply to this?* I was the world's worst guitarist, but I thought, *Yeah, I'll give that a go.* Even then I could see Rachel and Neil had something going on, and they wanted to take things in a more noisy direction.

Rachel Goswell: We advertised for a female guitarist, but Christian was the only person who replied. He said he would wear a dress if he needed to.

Christian Savill: I think the reason they let me join—because I was severely lacking in musical ability—is that we were really into the same music and we got on really well. We immediately had a shared vision for what we wanted to do.

Rachel Goswell: In the early stages, our tastes were quite mixed. Nick and I were the goths. Neil was into the Primitives and more "indie schmindie" stuff. Adrian was pretty straight-laced. Christian was just into the Valentines. I think we came together around a mutual appreciation of MBV, Jesus and Mary Chain, and Cocteau Twins.

Nick Chaplin: When we changed the name to Slowdive, we liked bands that had quite short names, like Lush or Loop. I think Rachel came up with it, but we made up the legend that I dreamt it because we didn't want to admit to Neil that it was a Siouxsie and the Banshees song. He was already embarrassed that he had two goths in his band.

As the only comparable band in the microscopic Reading scene, Slowdive naturally became the little brother to the already blossoming Chapterhouse.

Neil Halstead: Chapterhouse was the only other band around that had similar influences to us and were doing a similar kind of music.

Nick Chaplin: Chapterhouse had a much harder sound. I think we kind of envied them a bit, which pushed us in a different direction. We knew we couldn't compete on a level playing field, so we tried to make things a bit more orchestral while keeping the noise that really hits you in the gut.

Christian Savill: They kind of made us work harder by inspiring us and showing us the way. We were suddenly rehearsing all the time, playing a lot of gigs, and improving quite quickly. Then we got these songs together.

Rachel Goswell: We'd done a couple of songs that were more like direct MBV ripoffs. It was "Avalyn" where we sort of stumbled on that Slowdive sound.

Neil Halstead: Getting in the studio and discovering the reverb button really helped us find our sound. There was a moment when the engineer accidentally put reverb on everything, and we were all like, "Oh fuck, what did you just do?! Don't change it!" It w like there was a button that makes you sound cool.

Rachel Goswell: We did a support gig in Reading for a band called Five Thirty, and somebody from EMI Publishing was there who loved it.

Christian Savill: This guy came up to me and said, "I really liked your set. Have you got a demo tape?" I just thought he was some weird old hippie, so I said, "No, I haven't got one," but one of the guys from Five Thirty said, "You should go and get him a tape."

Neil Halstead: We'd literally just recorded a demo the week before, so Rachel scurried off back to our house, which was just around the corner from the After Dark Club, and grabbed a demo.

Rachel Goswell: We gave him a cassette that had "Slowdive" and "Avalyn" on it. He gave it to Alan McGee and the rest is history.

*

Rounding out the founding class of shoegaze bands, latecomers Moose formed in London around guitarists and best mates Russell Yates and K. J. "Moose" McKillop.

Moose McKillop: I got a job at the Record and Tape Exchange in London in the spring of 1989. On my first day, there I started working with a guy called Russell, and we hit it off absolutely immediately. By lunchtime, we were having a couple of beers together, and we went for more drinks after work. If it was a romantic thing, you'd call it love at first sight. We found that we had very similar tastes in music—'60s psych and folk like Love, Tim Buckley, and Nick Drake, lots of punk and new wave bands, plus reggae and jazz—it was quite uncanny.

In no time, this bromance started making beautiful, noisy music together that was, in many ways, the most refined of the bunch.

Moose McKillop: Within weeks of knowing each other, we decided that we'd try and form a band. There were a few friends that came along to early jamming sessions before we fixed on our original bass player, Jeremy Tishler, who also worked at Record and Tape. Damian Warburton, the original drummer, was a student at the same college as me, so it didn't take long to get things up and running.

As for the name, "Moose, the man" came before "Moose, the band."

Moose McKillop: At the college bar I used to go to, the cheapest beer on tap was a Canadian lager called Moosehead, so every time anybody asked, "Do you wanna drink?" I'd say, "Just get me a Moosehead." Moosehead became my nickname, and was then shortened to Moose. It was Russell who said, "That's a great name for a band," to which I said, "No, it's not. It's *my* nickname!" But Russell said, "Let's just go with it."

By the following summer of 1990—when the other main shoegazers were already releasing their first EPs—Moose recorded a demo tape and began playing their first live shows, before quickly getting signed to Hut Records with more than a little help from fellow London shoegazers Lush. (At the time Russell was dating Emma, while Moose eventually settled down with Miki.)

Moose McKillop: The best thing that happened was that Lush were doing a couple of spring gigs that year, and Emma and Miki said, "Why don't you support us at these shows?" At our second ever show, there was a journalist from the *NME*, and he reviewed us. That same night, we got approached by a couple of record labels who said, "Can you send us your demo? We'd love to speak to you." So our lucky break was handed to us on a plate. It couldn't have gone any better.

4 Shoegaze for Sale

As these bands began to find their footing and start recording demos, the notion of signing to a record label was suddenly an abstract reality. For the young shoegazers, two labels—Creation Records and 4AD—were more desirable than the rest, and thus became the labels associated with the shoegaze movement.

Christian Savill: To me there were two record labels in the UK that I was interested in: Creation and 4AD. They just had all the bands that I was really loving at that time, My Bloody Valentine and Cocteau Twins being the main ones. The Jesus and Mary Chain had started out on Creation, which also had the House of Love, Felt, and then Ride. 4AD also had Pixies. It sounds melodramatic now, but when you were eighteen and music was your life, these labels were everything.

Between the two beloved indies, Creation—which was inseparable from its boisterous boss and A&R man Alan McGee—would end up signing the most shoegaze bands.

Paul Lester: Creation was *the* shoegaze label.

Adam Franklin: From 1990 onwards, Alan McGee was like Chelsea Football Club, just hoovering up all the talent, which is when you get bands like Swervedriver, Slowdive, Teenage Fanclub, the Telescopes, and the Boo Radleys. It really is the label that spawned shoegaze.

Alan McGee: I mean, now shoegaze is a massive genre and it sounds kind of incredible that one person would sign all these bands, but at the time nobody else wanted these fucking bands. That's the truth.

Nick Chaplin: Alan is first and foremost a music fan. He is a good businessman too, but that's secondary. His skills were very much in picking up bands and motivating them to make better music.

Steve Queralt: Alan was always really encouraging. He was this very enthusiastic, larger-than-life character, and we felt that he was as excited about it as we were. I can remember Alan saying, "Look, there's no strings attached." There was no talk of a six-album deal tying us down for years and years. It was, "I just wanna put out this first EP and let's see what happens."

With McGee as their mad ringleader, Creation's London headquarters also acquired a well-earned reputation for debaucherous behavior.

Mark Gardener: Some of those Creation parties were legendary. We'd be partying with My Bloody Valentine and Primal Scream and the other bands on the label. You'd go in on Friday for a meeting, and then you'd come out on Monday, going, *I have no idea what happened in there*. It was great.

Adam Franklin: We normally made our excuses and left, but sometimes you'd get in there in the morning and there'd be people there hanging around from the previous day, who'd slept in cupboards.

Neil Halstead: We [in Slowdive] always felt like the babies of the label. It seemed like whenever we arrived at the offices, the party had just happened and the drugs got put away.

Alan McGee: I think I warned the people at the label not to give Slowdive drugs, which probably annoyed the band, but they were literally children.

Against the steep odds created by organizational chaos and risky business decisions, Creation managed to mostly do right by their bands.

Jimmy Hartridge: It was a really ramshackle organization. They got stuff done and had a press team who managed to get a lot of press, but they lived very much on a day-to-day basis. They'd spend too much money on something and then take somebody else's money to pay for it, but Alan didn't really care about the money. He was just driven by the power of the music. Everyone was.

For his part, 4AD boss Ivo Watts-Russell—and, by extension, the culture at his label—couldn't have been more different than that of rock and roll maverick Alan McGee.

Chris Roberts: Alan would be yapping at you, "Ride are brilliant! Ride are fantastic! You've gotta like Ride," almost sledge-hammering you until you caved in. Ivo was the opposite. He was quiet and reserved, but he spoke softly and carried a big influence. He would say, "I really quite like this band Throwing Muses" or "I think the new Cocteau Twins record is beautiful," and you'd believe him because he would choose his words.

Emma Anderson: It's quite good having your A&R person as the boss of the label, which is obviously not what you have at a major. Ivo was very much into the music and the final product, and not what's gonna sell. He was very supportive, he said what he felt, and when there were problems, he stepped in and tried to solve them.

Ian Masters: He was a very reserved Englishman with a very strong idea of where he wanted the label to go and what he wanted to achieve. He just wanted to give the music as good a chance as it could possibly have, given that it was being put out by a fairly small label. He didn't have the promotional budgets of the major labels, so I think he realized that the money that he spent had to really be well targeted to maximize every penny.

More than just almost any label like it, 4AD also had earned an ironclad reputation for both its high-quality roster, personally curated by Ivo, and the very specific look of its releases, credited to 23 Envelope—the two-man team of graphic designer Vaughan Oliver and photographer-filmmaker Nigel Grierson—which morphed into v23 when Grierson left in 1988 and was replaced by designer Chris Bigg.

Ian Masters: From the time that Cocteau Twins started putting out albums, 4AD started to get more and more people buying basically anything that came out on the label. Ivo Watts-Russell had a very eclectic taste in music, and coupling that with Vaughan Oliver's artwork, it acquired a very strong character. Starting with Cocteau Twins and the Birthday Party, and onto Pixies and Throwing Muses, that was really a golden period for them.

Miki Berenyi: With 4AD there was an aesthetic sensibility. People thought of 4AD as this ivory tower, and it was probably because of the artwork. They had 23 Envelope packaging everything. There was this mystique created by the fact that you rarely, if ever, saw the band's picture on the sleeves.

Steve Queralt: We were not only inspired by the music of the bands on Creation and 4AD, but also the aesthetic. It was how those bands marketed and projected themselves. Album sleeves were pieces of art. They didn't just stick a picture of the band on the cover with the word "Ride." There was more to it than that.

Despite their differences, both labels were essential to the movement they fostered for the same basic factors: their passionate A&R-first approach, their emphasis on aesthetics, and their willingness to support a band's creative vision over commercial concerns.

Andy Bell: Alan gave us complete creative freedom and always played it pretty straight with us. Creation was a label with a good ethos, as well as good music. Once you were signed, you could do what you wanted.

Miki Berenyi: I get a lot of questions about how sexist the music industry is, but half the people who worked at 4AD were women, and half the bands on 4AD had women in them. They didn't think of us as a girl band at all. We were just a band.

Neil Halstead: We've been on both labels [as Slowdive and Mojave 3], and we were always just left to our own devices. We were never told, "You've gotta do this or that."

Ian Masters: Especially after dealing with other labels afterwards, it was very, very positive. They really just made sure that we had good studios, good engineers, good marketing, and good promotion. Having put themselves behind the music, they were determined to present it in the most beautiful and inviting way.

While no label is perfect, and both Creation and 4AD would eventually make moves that hurt or upset some of their bands, hindsight confirms that they were the optimal place to be, especially in contrast to the so-called "fake indies" of the day— such as BMG subsidiary Dedicated Records and Virgin imprint Hut Records—who would scoop up bands like Chapterhouse, Moose, and Revolver, only to leave them high and dry down the road.

5 The Almighty Music Press

If you lived in the UK and cared about alternative music in the '80s and '90s, your options for learning about new bands were exceedingly limited. Without the internet, social media, or more than the rare plug on radio and TV, your world revolved around the handful of weekly print publications that told you which bands to follow and which records to buy. As such, for better and for worse, shoegaze as we know it would not exist without the British music press.

Stephen Patman: If you weren't within the mainstream music scene, there was no real outlet for you other than the music papers. John Peel might play you after ten at night, *120 Minutes* might play a video at three in the morning, but the music press really had a monopoly on how people found out about alternative music. They had a lot of power in that period of time, and they really fancied themselves because they knew they could mold the world.

Of the four major weeklies—*Sounds*, *Record Mirror*, *Melody Maker*, and *New Musical Express* (*NME*)—*Melody Maker* and *NME* were the most influential, and the two that primarily covered shoegaze, while *Sounds* and *Record Mirror* would shutter their doors in early 1991, just as shoegaze was reaching its zenith.

Nick Chaplin: We would go out and buy *Melody Maker* and the *NME* on the day they came out. It formed people's tastes and opinions without a doubt.

Alan McGee: The *NME* and the *Melody Maker* were kingmakers for a long time. I was good at working that to my advantage.

David Quantick (*NME*): *NME* has always been more of a laddish magazine—more friendly, more comedy, more of a poppy feel that appeals to students and teenagers. *Melody Maker* was a bit darker, more serious, and chin-stroking.

Andy Sherriff: We were definitely more of a *Melody Maker* band.

With so many papers, competition for readers and advertisers was intense. This was made all the more absurd by the fact that *Melody Maker* and *NME* were owned by the same publisher.

David Quantick: At this point, the *NME* was outselling *Melody Maker* by something like 80,000 to 20,000 copies. And the thing that everybody found ironically hilarious was that we were all in the same building, one floor apart from each other, so we used to see each other in the lift, drink in the same pub, and when one of us dies, we all go to each other's funerals.

Naturally, this competition—not to mention the wider British media's love for tabloid drama—bred a sensationalistic style of music journalism unmatched outside of the UK.

Steve Sutherland: Britain is a tiny island and there were four of these weekly papers vying for readers, so you can imagine the fierce competition around getting people on the front cover, discovering new things, and trying to get the best interviews and most outrageous reviews.

Polly Birkbeck (PR): It was very tongue-in-cheek, with headlines and captions that were always nudge-nudge jokes. They'd have a gossip column where they did take the piss out of a lot of bands. Some people thought it was real.

Sonic Boom: Every week these papers had to fill their pages with some other fluffed-up marshmallow fucking bullshit. It formed some sort of weird hype vortex where you could create a certain unreality quite quickly.

One of the ways they held readers' attention was by coining scenes, trends, and movements.

Steve Sutherland: In the UK we were very scene driven, and the writers and photographers wanted to make a reputation on discovering stuff, so they were always looking for the next thing to excite readers.

Polly Birkbeck: *Melody Maker* and *NME* were always trying to create a scene each. *NME* was invariably more successful.

David Quantick: Every week there was an endless supply of new musical movements, such as the "new wave of new wave" and "shambling," some of which were real.

Needless to say, when the music papers started sniffing out a trend among these buzzing bands who were (1) made in the image of My Bloody Valentine and the Cocteau Twins, (2) largely signed to the same labels, and (3) could sometimes be found socializing at the same shows and pubs, they were ready to pounce.

Steve Sutherland: It was such a small scene, but because the journalists all hung out with the bands in the same clubs and gigs, it was very easy to amplify a very small thing into a very big thing for the readership, and then record companies started sniffing around.

Chris Roberts: A band's audience would quadruple after a good review. We were basically doing the A&R men's jobs. We'd do a live review of some band in a tiny pub in South London, and at their next gig there would be loads of A&R men in there.

David Quantick: Often when we made up a scene, it would be a little bit incoherent, but shoegaze *was* a coherent scene. If you played these records, you could put all these bands on a compilation or mixtape and it would sound great, whereas with Britpop, we were very much lumping in Blur, Pulp, and Oasis, and it sounded hellish.

Paul Lester: The great thing about shoegaze was that it was a blank canvas that journalists could scrawl all over. The writing about these groups was just so over the top. Each week they were trying to outdo each other and reach new heights in the album reviews and live reviews. As new groups would come along, you'd be like, *Oh, great, we can try another series of ridiculously fanciful rock writing*. Chris Roberts, even by the standards of *Melody Maker*, was almost the final word. You couldn't really go beyond what he wrote 'cause it was just so ridiculously fawning.

Chris Roberts: The whole thing was very accelerated. Ride went from playing tiny venues to winning the readers' poll for best band one year later, and the paper got behind it. We all did. It was very much a herd mentality at that time. You could disagree with the party line, but it made sense to say, "Here's a new movement. Let's champion it and get this one rolling."

6 Shoegaze Rising

In the compact history of shoegaze releases, 1990 was surely the year the movement started to walk on its own two feet. That said, it took its first steps in the autumn of 1989.

While Alan McGee was signing Ride and Swervedriver to Creation, Chapterhouse was solidifying its lineup, and Slowdive and Moose were barely coming together, 4AD got the ball rolling with the September 1989 release of Pale Saints' first EP, *Barging Into the Presence of God*—boasting the angelic opener "Sight of You"—followed by Lush's debut release, the six-song mini-album, *Scar*—which joined the band's three original demos with three new songs. In addition to being produced by 4AD favorite John Fryer (who also worked on the first two Cocteau Twins albums), both releases were quickly acclaimed by the UK press and both hit number 3 on the UK Indie Chart. In a gushing review for *NME*, Simon Williams called *Scar* "a work of art" while claiming of their dualistic sound, "Few other bands can blend melody and malevolence so flawlessly."[1]

Appropriately, the two 4AD bands played a co-headlining show in Leeds that December. In a live review of the gig for *Melody Maker*, Dave Simpson was less than impressed with either hyped outfit, especially young Lush, who had by then earned an unfortunate reputation for their abysmal early performances, calling out their "ham-fisted guitar," "stumbling vocals," "muddy mix," and "trembling nerves."[2] As for Pale Saints,

Simpson faulted their sometimes clumsy and rushed delivery while commending their inviting sonics: "a Mary Chain-meets-Phil Spector waterfall of shrieking melody . . . urgent dynamics, thundering drums and cutting guitars. They have an aura about them, an unmistakable air of the driven."

Following that 1989 prelude, shoegaze's breakthrough year began bright and early in 1990. Leading the pack, both in terms of timing and popularity, was Ride, who would manage to release three fantastic EPs and a genre-defining album before Christmas, beginning with the four-track *Ride* EP on January 15. The record was buoyed by a happenstance appearance on *Snub TV*, which was filming Galaxie 500 at a West London gig where they were booked as support.

Mark Gardener: They filmed us doing "Drive Blind" live and put it out on television the night our EP was released. That really helped give it a bump.

"Ride are almost too perfect, too great to be true," wrote Chris Roberts in a two-page spread in *Melody Maker*. "This is the only criticism I can make of their astonishing debut EP. Not only do they harness the inspirational guitar whirlwinds of My Bloody Valentine, Spacemen 3 and Loop, then unleash it on classic, doomed, romantic pop songs, they are also young and petulantly pretty and knock me through the wall live."[3]

Jane Savidge: When I saw Ride in my twenties, I thought, *These are my Beatles. These are the indie Beatles.*

In the same feature, as if sowing the seeds of the scene they would soon be cast into, an unspecified member of the band claims, "The Nineties are going to be great. There are lots of bands doing new things with guitars. The Pale Saints and Lush are way apart from us, but perhaps there is a similarity in approach. Which is weird. It's almost like a generation's gone and now there's a new generation."

A month later Pale Saints unleashed their debut full-length, *The Comforts of Madness*. With its psychedelic Vaughan Oliver artwork, '60s grooves and harmonies, and rich and fuzzy textures, it's a brilliant stepping stone between the dream pop of the Cocteau Twins and the more violent sounds of shoegaze to come, which *NME's* Simon Williams called an "unnervingly multi-dimensional collage of melody and friction" with "absolutely no stinkers."[4]

Hot on their heels was Lush, who quickly eclipsed their recent mini-album with the *Mad Love* EP, produced by none other than Robin Guthrie, who became something of a mentor to the band.

Miki Berenyi: Robin really clicked with the band. He came and saw us on tour. When we did a Peel session, he came along. So he was really keen on the whole thing, and it was a real thrill for us to be working with him.

Robin Guthrie: I'd made a few records already by that time, so I was kind of in my groove. They were just a baby band then, so maybe I gave them a bit of confidence and more precision.

In a February feature story for *Melody Maker*, Steve Sutherland hailed *Mad Love* as "a beautiful, primitive record" that charted a new, forward-looking course for pop music while shedding their early reputation as a crappy live act who hadn't earned their hype.[5]

That April saw the release of Ride's second EP, *Play*, which peaked at number 32 in the UK singles chart and was combined with the *Ride* EP and released as the *Smile* mini-album in the United States. Three weeks later came My Bloody Valentine's first release since *Isn't Anything*, the *Glider* EP.

Opening with the blissful, breakbeat-driven earworm "Soon"—which Brian Eno would famously call "the vaguest music ever to have been a hit"[6] after it reached number 2 on the UK Indie Chart—Chris Roberts lauded *Glider* as "completely different, utterly compelling, and again indisputably transcendent" in an interview with the band.[7] When asked about the numerous My Bloody Valentine "clones" that had emerged since their last album, Kevin Shields generously observed, "I genuinely believe that unless you're a genius you have to be derivative first to get to know how to be original." Amusingly, the article also claims the band's next LP was "nearly finished," though it would end up being another eighteen months before *Loveless* arrived.

By July, Creation Records was firing on all cylinders with Swervedriver's debut four-track EP, *Son of Mustang Ford*. Calling the title track "a chromium-plated piece of automobile romanticism," *Melody Maker*'s Simon Price described the band's heavy, American sound by asking the reader to imagine Dinosaur Jr. playing "Bat Out Of Hell" or Hüsker Dü playing "Born To Run."[8] Similarly, *NME*'s Simon Williams called the Oxford foursome "tightrope walkers" for how they juxtaposed in-your-face riffs with Valentinesy atmospheres, writing, "*Son Of Mustang Ford* is the sound of a band grubbying Creation's clean-cut history . . . taking contemporary American guitar rock and instilling it with a liberal dose of languid British dreampop."[9]

At the same time, and with a similarly American angle on the shoegaze sound, northern noisemakers the Boo Radleys also released their debut album, *Ichabod and I*, on Action Records. Though little-noticed by the press and never re-released, it got them briefly signed to the soon-to-fail (and subsequently revived) Rough Trade Records, before eventually being scooped up by Creation.

In September, after three years of patiently gigging around London, Chapterhouse made their belated debut with the *Freefall* EP, featuring the hypnotic opener "Falling Down." "Chapterhouse ooze style," wrote Cathi Unsworth in a story for *Sounds*. "They don't just look it, they live it, and the three-guitar heaven of their music has all the right elements of sex, disenchantment and hedonism to make them so much cooler than the rest."[10]

In that same article, Unsworth points out the band's annoyance at the increasingly crowded field of noisy guitar bands, writing,

> At the start of this year, Chapterhouse were ready to unleash themselves on a public that had yet to get automated to either Swervedriver or Ride. And now, despite sounding very little like either, they feel considerably miffed at being beaten to top of the Wah Wah Gods league by the age old hassle of "getting the right record deal."

Showing no mercy, Ride dropped their third EP, *Fall*, the following week, which they followed up a month later with their monumental full-length, *Nowhere*, both of which the

NME's Roger Morton compared to the first two EPs by saying, "The songs are deeper, larger in scale and mostly less dirty sounding, but the balance of noise and melody, nihilism and amazement, is perfectly preserved."[11]

Mark Gardener: I guess it was a lot of music to put out at that time, but it didn't really feel like it. The momentum was good and we just kept going with writing and recording.

Steve Queralt: I still find it hard to believe that we put out three EPs, but we were so confident in the amount of music we had to put out. Even Creation was asking us if we were sure we wanted to put so much music out so quickly, and *did we have anything left for an album?*

Of course, this seemingly bottomless tap of songwriting energy came largely at the expense of their sleep schedules and their producer's mental health.

Steve Queralt: *Nowhere* was recorded very, very quickly. I think we had to finish it in two weeks, and that included recording and mixing. When we'd recorded our demos, the engineer was a guy called Marc Waterman, and we liked him so much that we gave him no choice when we said to him, "You're gonna produce our album." So we took him into Blackwing Studios to record, but when it came to mixing, I think we'd blown his ears off.

Mark Gardener: We were just working through the night every night. You can do that quite easily when you are eighteen or nineteen, but he was under a lot of pressure and we realized he wasn't gonna be able to mix the record. McGee was always around us, and he realized we needed some help.

Alan McGee: When they first recorded *Nowhere*, it sounded pretty terrible. So I called up Alan Moulder.

At the time, producer Alan Moulder was just starting out his career, but having freshly engineered the Jesus and Mary Chain's *Automatic* and My Bloody Valentine's *Glider* EP, McGee figured he might be the right man to make sense of Ride's dark and stormy sound.

Steve Queralt: He kind of came in at the eleventh hour and saved the day.

The end result is one of shoegaze's finest statements. *Nowhere* is as fierce and focused as it is contemplative and chaotic, from the runaway train of "Seagull" and the harrowing march of "Dreams Burn Down" to the heartbreakingly sentimental "Vapour Trail."

Mark Gardener: We were definitely still boys when we made that record. There's a beautiful naïveté, angst, and darkness about it that reflects that period when we'd first left home for art school, feeling like outsiders in that weird town, living in dodgy conditions, and first falling in love and getting dumped. It really fueled us all to use the band as a way out of this darkness to better times.

Alan Moulder: When people describe shoegaze, *Nowhere* pretty much ticks all the boxes.

Interestingly, though the album is retrospectively regarded as a masterpiece—holding the number 3 spot on *Pitchfork*'s "50 Best Shoegaze Albums of All Time"[12]—enthusiasm was more measured at the time, perhaps due to the insurmountably high expectations they'd created with their meteoric ascent.

"In a sense, Ride have dug their own graves," wrote Simon Williams. "They've already astonished us with 'Drive Blind' and 'Taste'. . . . Now we want them to achieve the virtually impossible and transcend their own transcendence. Brutally unfair, really."[13] Sharing those sentiments Chris Roberts wrote, "Ride's much-anticipated debut album . . . isn't quite the empire of the senses we'd been polishing our boots and praying for. It's full of noble ideas and every guitar sound under and over the sun, but it doesn't really gell [sic] as a great LP."[14]

It's worth pausing to mention that while there were certainly other important producers in shoegaze, none have had their name so attached to the sound as Alan Moulder, whose engineering, mixing, and production credits include genre milestones like My Bloody Valentine's Loveless, Ride's Nowhere, and Swervedriver's Mezcal Head, as well as various releases by Lush, Slowdive, Curve, and the Boo Radleys. From those shoegazey beginnings, he has gone on to work his studio magic on records by the Smashing Pumpkins, Nine Inch Nails, the Cure, U2, the Killers, Foo Fighters, Yeah Yeah Yeahs, and Beach House.

Alan McGee: Alan's amazing. Brilliant fucking producer and engineer. Solid gold individual.

Adam Franklin: When you're dealing with these stupidly loud guitar bands, you listen to it back and it's sort of sludge. Alan would say, "Right guys, go to the pub next door, come back in half an hour," and he'd find somewhere to position all these things in the mix. You would come back and be like,

Fucking hell! We can actually hear all these guitar parts that we imagined in our heads, and Alan Moulder made it come to life. That's why he was the one engineer that Kevin Shields trusted. His influence is immeasurable.

Alan Moulder: The thing I love about shoegaze is the beauty and the violence. That's right up my street. It was really exciting because we were all in the same age group and still inexperienced, so we were all learning together. I was probably a more sympathetic ear than most of the older engineers who were set in their ways. My job was more a case of trying to get what was in their heads to come out of the speakers.

On top of *Nowhere* hitting record stores on that day, October 15 marked two other noteworthy releases. First, there was Lush's *Sweetness and Light* EP, whose heavenly title track represents a high watermark of shoegaze's pop potential—even if *Melody Maker* thought it was "sorely over-produced."[15] The second was Blur's debut single, "She's So High," which, while not ethereal or noisy enough to be called straight shoegaze, is evidence of the genre's early influence on the future Britpoppers who were regulars on the shoegaze social scene.

Rounding out the year, November saw the release of Swervedriver's *Rave Down* EP—which bassist Adi Vines described as "ethereal metal" after it earned them praise in a heavy metal magazine[16]—Chapterhouse's *Sunburst* EP—featuring the original version of "Something More," later reworked by Robin Guthrie, and their fast and fuzzed-out cover of the Beatles'"Rain"—and, most significantly, Slowdive's debut *Slowdive* EP, which raked in rave reviews from *NME* and *Melody Maker*, earning the latter's coveted "Single of the Week" badge.

By the end of 1990, shoegaze was shaping into a recognizable alternative music phenomenon, even if it didn't yet have a name. With their whirlwind output, Ride was front and center, which John Peel seemed to recognize by including three of their songs on his year-end Festive Fifty list.[17] It's worth noting that, despite the hoopla, shoegaze was still an underground sensation in an eclectic field that also featured popular releases from Madchester (Happy Mondays, the Charlatans), electronica (the KLF, Saint Etienne), American indie (Pixies, Breeders), dance (Deee-Lite, Beats International), and hip-hop (Public Enemy, Stereo MC's). Thus, in *Melody Maker*'s year-end critics poll, only *Nowhere* placed in their Top 30 albums of 1990 (#20), while their year-end list of singles included My Bloody Valentine's *Glider* EP (#5), Ride's *Fall* EP (#7), and Lush's *Mad Love* EP (#19).[18] Of course, once shoegaze did eventually break out, some bands would be wishing it would have stayed subterranean.

7 The Scene That Celebrates Itself

When these noisy guitar bands from the Thames Valley and beyond found themselves releasing records and regularly gigging, they quickly outgrew their hometowns. For most, it only made sense to move to London, where the action was. And as is only natural when you like the same music and are signed to the same few labels, the bands found themselves increasingly running into each other.

Nick Chaplin: It was such a good time for guitar bands with our background. There were so many of us about, we were on a handful of labels, and every night there was a really good band to go and see—and so we would tend to hang out.

Moose McKillop: Parts of London can seem like a village. You could walk into certain pubs, clubs, or venues on your own, and within twenty minutes you had hooked up with half a dozen people from various bands. The next thing you knew, you were all drunk and staggering home.

Jimmy Hartridge: Everybody did move to London, and even though it's a big city, you find the same people at the same gigs, influencing each other, just like you had in the '60s, but on a smaller scale. I don't know how you define a movement, but I suppose if you hang out with people, get to know them, and you are playing music that you all like, then there's the movement.

Some of the more well-known meeting points were Syndrome, a weekly indie music club hosted in a basement bar in Oxford Street, and venues like the Camden Falcon, the Borderline, the Powerhaus, and the Underworld. Outside of London, the shoegazers also found themselves being booked on tours with each other. When the music papers inevitably took note, it was only a matter of time before it was given a name and sensationalized.

Steve Sutherland: The Scene That Celebrates Itself. I was the one who created that mad idea.

Emma Anderson: It was a bit exaggerated. I mean we all lived in London, and we used to sometimes go to the same gigs, but it wasn't like we all lived in the same house or were hanging out day and night. Sometimes we'd be at the bar, and a photographer would be there and take a photo of me, Stephen from Chapterhouse, and Alex from Blur—so the papers would say, "Oh look, they're all hanging out together."

Chris Roberts: Everyone would be getting drunk [at Syndrome], including some of us journalists. But because the gossip columns had so little to comment on, it would read, "One of Ride, one of Lush, and one of Chapterhouse were spotted at Syndrome on Thursday." And then if two people started dating, that *definitely* got in the gossip column. It was totally absurd and comical to be making hay out of these tiny indie bands that were barely making a living, but it all added to the sense of momentum that there was a scene.

Robin Guthrie: It's kinda strange how the popular imagination seems to have this idea of everybody hanging out and having some scene together. It's like, *No, just because we were on the same label as other bands doesn't mean we were all friends with each other, like one big family*. There were some fantastic people, but I found quite a lot of the music unlistenable.

Depending on who you ask, the long-winded term, often called "The Scene" for short, was taken as a sarcastic jab.

Sonic Boom: It's like they were saying, *Well, the only people who go to any of these shows are all the other bands, so it's a scene that celebrates itself*, which was a journalist trying to be mean, really.

Paul Lester: It was a fun, tongue-in-cheek, mildly damning sobriquet.

Simon Scott: It seemed to be a bit of a slight, but we just ignored that stuff.

Nick Chaplin: It just became another stick to beat everybody with.

To others, including the man who coined it, the term was complimenting what made the scene unique and endearing.

Miki Berenyi: Steve Sutherland has argued since that he meant it as a nice term, like, *Oh look, these bands who name check each other, turn up to each other's gigs, and lend each other gear. They're mates!* Which is contrary to the usual backbiting that you get between bands.

Steve Sutherland: If you look it up on Wikipedia, it's interpreted as a snarky critique. But it wasn't! It just captured my feeling that every time you went to see these bands, all the other bands were there, which was very unusual then.

Christian Savill: It definitely pissed people off, but I didn't have a problem with it because I thought it was really lovely that you had like-minded people who you could hang out with.

Alan Moulder: No one really slagged each other off. Everyone was open and appreciative of what each other were doing. I got the sense that the '60s was a bit like that. The Beatles and the Stones were probably very competitive, but there was mutual respect.

Neil Halstead: It was a genuinely supportive scene. All the bands would try and support the other bands and be at their gigs and talk about them in interviews. It was a nice thing that the music press took the piss out of.

So who actually was included in The Scene That Celebrates Itself? For starters, you have our core group of shoegazers: Slowdive, Ride, Swervedriver, Chapterhouse, Lush, and Moose. But beyond them, The Scene also included the likes of avant-pop group Stereolab—who often swapped members with Moose and lesser-known noise act Th' Faith Healers— and a young Blur. Also frequently lumped in by the press were shoegazey bands like Catherine Wheel, Curve, Cranes, Silverfish, and Pale Saints, whether or not they had any meaningful connection to the London club scene.

Ian Masters: Being based in Leeds, we were so geographically distant from what was going on in London. The only time that we would see other bands in London was when we came down to do our own gigs or to meet people at 4AD, so we felt pretty isolated.

Eventually, the odd American band was even thrown into the mix. When first visiting the UK to meet with labels in 1991, Greg Ackell of Boston shoegaze band Drop Nineteens remembers first experiencing The Scene in its most idealized version.

Greg Ackell (Drop Nineteens): Stephen and Andy from Chapterhouse reached out and offered me to stay with them in London. We went to some shows, and it was all the proverbial bands at the time: Moose, Lush, Cranes, Pale Saints, Chapterhouse, Ride, Slowdive. You could see one of those bands playing almost every other night. I remember my first night in London, I was at a party after one of those shows, and I met Mark from Ride, Neil and Rachel from Slowdive, Miki and Emma from Lush, the Reid brothers from the Jesus and Mary Chain, and even Robin Guthrie and Liz Fraser were there. All those people were talking about us, everyone was very supportive of one another, and they just invited us in.

One band that definitely *wasn't* part of The Scene was reclusive shoegaze demigods My Bloody Valentine.

Neil Halstead: MBV were a bit more aloof. We certainly never hung out with them. We would've been totally in awe of them.

In the end, being grouped into The Scene That Celebrates Itself was both a blessing and a curse, in that it both elevated a band who may have been ignored on their own while limiting their ability to define themselves on their own terms. Regardless of the upsides, most bands rejected the attempt at being categorized.

Chris Roberts: A band like Chapterhouse got pulled into the magnetic force of shoegaze. They wanted to succeed, but they had mixed feelings about getting caught up in a genre. They strained at the leash—like Lush did, like Ride did—because they didn't want to be pigeonholed.

Miki Berenyi: Most scenes were invented to sell papers. It's fine for the My Bloody Valentines, who are heralded as the geniuses of it, but not so great for everybody else who's seen as substandard to that. It knocks off all your interesting edges. I get how you can compare Swervedriver to Chapterhouse, but it's quite tenuous.

Robin Guthrie: First Cocteau Twins was post-punk, then we were dream pop, and then shoegaze. All these different fucking names would come along and it changed all the time. I never tried to put myself in the same movement or scene as other bands. I just never identified with that.

Ian Masters: It didn't really bother me to be written about as part of that scene. It was lazy soundbite journalism, but any press is good press, as they say, and the only time you really need to worry is when you're not getting written about at all.

David Quantick: Bands hate to be part of a scene because being part of a scene means you're not original. Goth bands are hilarious, because if you say to Nick Cave, Siouxsie Sioux, or Robert Smith, "You're a goth band," they'll say, "No, we're not!" *So who is then?* Don't believe bands. Bands are the ones who say, "This is our greatest album" about some piece of crap that is nowhere near as good as their first single. Bands lie.

8 Shoegaze Peaking

If shoegaze had a golden year, when it was the talk of the town and all the bands were at their peak, it was unquestionably 1991. Following their whirlwind year of 1990, Ride started out on top again. Having won *Melody Maker*'s end-of-year reader's poll for best band, the subsequent January cover story declared them "Your Brightest Hope for a Grand New Year."[1]

Loz Colbert: It was just a big wave of activity that seemed to carry us forward into the new year. It felt like we had landed as a fully formed band, and it didn't stop.

Steve Queralt: We did a lot of touring as well, playing something like a hundred dates that first year. No wonder *Melody Maker* and *NME* were watching us, because you couldn't really escape it.

In early February, perhaps as a way to placate the impatience for My Bloody Valentine's continually delayed next album, Creation released their four-song *Tremolo* EP. Side A tracks "To Here Knows When" and "Swallow" showcased the band's newfound experimentation with sampling, with Kevin Shields admitting in an interview it took six weeks of trial and error to end up with the low-rumbling background noise on the first track—based on a stock sound of an explosion from the BBC.[2]

Two weeks later Creation dropped Slowdive's *Morningrise* EP, their only release to feature short-lived drummer Neil

Carter, who had already been replaced by Simon Scott. "The result is a mutant orchestral beauty, closer to left-field film soundtracks than Lush or The Boo Radleys," wrote *Melody Maker*'s Bob Stanley, continuing, "Slowdive won't be happy until they've found that elusive chord progression that makes you weep instantly at its beauty. On 'She Calls' and, especially, 'Losing Today', they've come damn close."[3]

The first week of March witnessed the debut releases of both Moose (*Jack* EP) and Curve (*Blindfold* EP). With shoegaze fever on the rise, influential PR firms like Savage & Best, who would later shape the Britpop movement, made a point of connecting new bands to the increasingly talked-about scene.

Jane Savidge: I definitely attached Moose, Curve, and Lush to this movement I saw springing up, even if bands disliked being put into them.

Hailing the *Jack* EP's emotional resonance and "gorgeous brutality," *Melody Maker*'s Mat Smith went on to say of Moose, "Although illuminated by the fast evaporating slipstream left by the Valentines, they're not choking on it in a welter of absurdly shallow psychedelics like so many of their contemporaries, but are criss-crossing the vapour trail with the sensual caresses of the Cocteaus and the controlled ambience of AR Kane."[4] In that same article, the band's painfully introverted demeanor is made clear when they admit they find interviews "egotistical" and that "overwhelmingly shy" Russell is only the singer because nobody else would, with Smith musing how their reluctance for attention "makes Slowdive look like David Lee Roth."

The *NME* was less impressed, with reviewer James Brown (no relation) shit-talking, "The guitars sound like a spookier House of Love but the singer, Russell, moans like he's got pubic hair caught round his epiglottis. C'mon, get some phlegm in your jaw before you start ruining your music with such tawdry vocals. Pedestrian and about as subversive as toothpaste."[5]

Though Curve would never be fully fledged figures in the shoegaze club—due mainly to Toni Halliday's bright vocals and their interesting fusion of hard techno production—the massive display of layered guitar distortion, not to mention the frequent production work of Halliday's future husband Alan Moulder, more than qualify them as partial members. Calling the *Blindfold* EP "simply and easily the most brilliant and surprising record we've heard in well over a year," the Stud Brothers' *Melody Maker* review calls each of the four tracks "an astonishingly great popsong," continuing, "Like Ride, the only real comparison that springs to mind, Curve can demolish and rebuild themselves in the course of one song. And, like Ride, they do write real songs."[6]

On the same day, Ride released their fourth EP, *Today Forever*, which shot up to number 14 on the UK charts. A week later, the band was invited to go where no shoegaze band had ever gone, and where no other shoegaze band would ever go: *Top of the Pops*.

Jimmy Hartridge: When Ride got on *Top of the Pops*, the TV show, it was unbelievable. I mean, that just didn't happen, and when Ride actually did, people started thinking, *Wow, maybe some of these bands could go somewhere.*

Nick Chaplin: A small indie band appearing on *Top of the Pops* was a huge deal. In the early '90s, it was still a massively important thing to do.

Alan Moulder: You get a band like that at their peak, where everyone's just coming up with stuff constantly, it was really exciting to see their trajectory. You really thought you were doing something unique managing to get bands like that on *Top of the Pops*.

Steve Queralt: Playing the show was a bit of a childhood dream when you started a band, and it's a way of showing your mom and dad, *This is why I left my job and joined a band*. It suddenly crossed over into their world and made sense to them.

As much as Ride's appearance on Britain's most watched music program represented shoegaze infiltrating the mainstream, the following week's charts revealed the apparent ceiling for how high shoegaze was able to climb.

Steve Queralt: Traditionally, you would go on *Top of the Pops* that Thursday, and people would flood to the shops and buy your single the very next day, so that you would find yourself at a higher position the next week. But when we did *Top of the Pops*, we immediately bombed out of the charts the following week, because the masses weren't interested in listening to our music.

Mark Gardener: Our fan base was so loyal that they all rushed out and bought our stuff as soon as we put them out, which is how we got on *Top of the Pops* in the first place.

Despite the unlikeliness of a shoegaze band on *Top of the Pops*, Ride would manage to repeat the feat less than a year later with "Leave Them All Behind," as well as a third time with 1994s "Birdman," which snuck into the Top 40 at number 38.

Mark Gardener: With "Leave Them All Behind" I think we entered the charts at number 9, which was higher than Michael Jackson at that time. It was like, *What?* It felt like we were invading a pop music space that wasn't our real place to be.

March 18 marked the release of Kitchens of Distinction's seminal second album, *Strange Free World*. Although not members of The Scene and discounted from "the Sound" mainly by Patrick Fitzgerald's Morrissey-meets-Ian McCulloch singing style, Julian Swales' swelling guitar work is undeniably influenced by the guitar pedal zeitgeist, and the album is thus considered by some to be a shoegaze classic.

Also on that day, and capping off their trio of EPs leading up to their full-length debut, Chapterhouse dropped the *Pearl* EP. Featuring swooning backup vocals from Slowdive's Rachel Goswell and a Madchester-influenced drum pattern based on a sped-up sample of John Bonham's iconic drumming on "When the Levee Breaks," title track "Pearl" stands alongside Lush's "Sweetness and Light" and My Bloody Valentine's "Soon" as one of shoegaze's most enduringly pop-friendly[7] specimens. Once again, *NME*'s James Brown was not a fan, hurling a few personal insults at the band before calling "Pearl" "a sleepwalking sort of song . . . which almost flowers into something quite pretty."

A month later, Chapterhouse's full-length album, *Whirlpool*, hit record stores. Featuring the previously released EP standouts "Pearl," "Falling Down," and "Something More"—the latter given a more polished remix by Robin Guthrie—the album spent three weeks on the UK Albums Chart and went on to be one of the year's biggest indie sellers, not to mention one of shoegaze's strongest LPs.

The next two months marked the release of Mercury Rev's debut album *Yourself Is Steam*, an early example of shoegaze's distinct guitar noise seeping into the American indie rock landscape. It also saw a slew of excellent shoegaze EPs, including Catherine Wheel's *Painful Thing* (which reached number 5 on the Indie Chart), Pale Saints' *Flesh Balloon* (marking the addition of original Lush vocalist Meriel Barham to the band), Slowdive's *Holding Our Breath* (earning the band its third consecutive "Single of the Week"), and Swervedriver's *Sandblasted* (lovingly described by Steve Sutherland as "a head-on collision between guitars raging for chaos" that "encompasses both the world-weary and the wonderstruck").[8]

In late July, the shoegaze faithful migrated an hour west of London, at the gateway to the Thames Valley, for the 1991 Slough Festival, or as it has since been called, "Shoegaze Woodstock." Headlined by Ride and featuring Slowdive, the bill was truthfully only half shoegaze if you count Curve and newcomers Revolver—whose debut EP included "Heaven Sent an Angel," which topped the Indie Chart that summer. Giving credence to The Scene That Celebrates Itself, however, the fest was also attended by members of Lush and Chapterhouse, which was of course faithfully reported on by the press.

That summer, with the wind of their high-charting *Whirlpool* LP at their backs and another great EP, *Mesmerise*, in the chamber, Chapterhouse embarked on a massive national tour where they played seemingly every mid-sized venue in the United Kingdom, topped off by appearances at their hometown's massive Reading Festival and Rotterdam's Ein Abend In Wien festival. At both fests, Chapterhouse was billed just below their heroes Sonic Youth and Dinosaur Jr., and just above a scrappy young trio from outside Seattle who were just weeks away from releasing their major label debut. At the latter gig, they decided to check out this little outfit called Nirvana.

Andy Sherriff: They played a couple of tracks off the upcoming album, and I just thought, *Wow, they're gonna be huge. This is gonna blow up.*

Less than a month later, in the midst of their first US tour, Chapterhouse found themselves again playing with Nirvana—this time at Boston radio station WFNX's eighth Birthday Bash—along with Smashing Pumpkins, who'd released their debut album, *Gish*, that May. The very next day, *Nevermind* was unleashed upon the world, altering the alternative music landscape forever.

Nirvana represented the fully distilled version of a sound that had been brewing in the Pacific Northwest for years— one not dissimilar from shoegaze in its pairing of powerful, distortion-drenched guitar and clear melodies, but much more primal and direct, and without the delicate flourishes or effeminate vocals. And once "Smells Like Teen Spirit" was let out of the lab, grunge fever quickly escalated to a global pandemic, pushing all other forms of rock to the side.

Nick Chaplin: We were well and truly knocked off whatever perch we were on by the Nirvanas of this world, and if you're gonna be knocked off by somebody, I suppose there's no one better. The music press started idolizing the "American invasion" of these Sub Pop and Pacific Northwest bands, who all started to get a much bigger profile than we did.

Andy Sherriff: I remember there being a massive shift in the culture. Everyone went mad on Nirvana, and then all these bands like Pearl Jam, who weren't as good and didn't seem that alternative.

Steve Sutherland: Grunge was perfect for the music press because you've got very traditional heroes playing very traditional roles, with victims and junkies and hard rock and long hair and Courtney Love. It was like a soap opera.

Andy Bell: Over the course of one year, it seemed like our kind of bands were getting a lot of coverage in the music papers, and then it was all about Mudhoney and Nirvana.

Mark Gardener: We were doing a lot of touring around the world, and it was only when we came back to England that this "shoegazing" phrase came up as a put-down from the English press. Nirvana changed the world as everyone knew it, and it made what we were doing seem a little less powerful, and a bit more "shoegazey."

The same month that Nirvana dropped the grunge A-bomb, Creation released Slowdive's debut full-length, *Just for a Day*. In stark contrast to the universal praise the band had received since their first EP, the album's tepid reception marked the first visible crack in the shoegaze levee. But to be fair, the band would be the first to tell you it wasn't their strongest showing.

Simon Scott: Neil was like, "I don't want any singles on it. I just want us to go into the studio and see what happens."

Neil Halstead: We didn't have any songs at all. We basically wrote, recorded, and mixed the album in six weeks. McGee literally had to get down on his knees and beg us to put "Catch the Breeze" on it. For me, it's the weakest record we did. In fact, I probably haven't listened to it since before it came out.

In a reversal of the usual dynamics, *NME* was actually complimentary of the album, with Simon Williams calling it "a fine, fragrant affair which should be allowed to stand and swoon on its own two feet."[9] Shoegaze champions *Melody Maker*, meanwhile, took the opposite stance. In a review titled "Dive Bomb," Paul Lester went out of his way to express his profound disappointment in what he'd hoped to be "the finest album of 1991," only to conclude that "a mixture of weary lethargy . . . and gross overconfidence have conspired to make it one of the year's drearier achievements."[10] Citing Ride's *Nowhere* and Chapterhouse's *Whirlpool* as previous letdowns, Lester openly wondered if these overhyped bands could hack the LP format. Finally, as if summoning the near constant negativity that Slowdive would continue to face afterward, he finished, "It's sad, because many of us were quick to celebrate the band's initial bursts of splendour. Now we're queuing up to administer a good kicking."

Paul Lester: I remember the lady at Creation sending me a sort of snippy note saying, "Did you not sleep well last night?"

And I'm thinking, *No, I genuinely don't think this is a very good album*, but I think she was probably right in a sense. It seemed like their moment had slightly passed.

Christian Savill: It got pretty personal and nasty. I was at Reading Festival when Paul Lester, who'd written some really lovely reviews for our early live shows and EPs, came over and said, "Look, I'm really sorry, but I'm doing the review of your album, and I really don't like the record." I was like, "Oh, okay. That's fine." And then this other *Melody Maker* journalist came over and was like, "Yeah, you'll be stacking shelves again in six weeks." I didn't even know who he was, and he just seemed to be taking so much delight in having that power to say, "Your band is finished."

Paul Lester: To hear that now is absolutely mortifying. I was young and I want to apologize to all of them individually, *and* to their parents and their children. Imagine the amount of work that would've gone into that record, and to just dismiss it in that way, it's just stupid.

Simon Scott: It's strange. They kind of go mad for you, and you are just thinking, *Well, this can't be true.* There was this frenzy of shoegaze becoming very popular, but it really quickly bottomed out. They were like, *Fuck that, we've just heard Nevermind*, and they very quickly tried to bury all those bands.

Perhaps due to their grungy sound, Swervedriver fared much better upon the release of their own debut full-length, *Raise*. Calling the album "incurably romantic" and conjuring of "the sound of the wheels spinning the second before you release the brake," Steve Sutherland praised the band while seemingly distancing them from the scene they were associated with, writing in *Melody Maker*, "*Raise* is a great road movie for the ears and a postcard sent back from the edge to those who cast an eye over Swervedriver's origins, lazily lumped them in with The Scene . . . and then ignored them."[11]

Meanwhile, after spending most of the year on the road and punting their debut album into next year, Lush dropped their first and only release of 1991, the Robin Guthrie-produced *Black Spring* EP. Though the record hit number 2 on the Indie Chart, its release was overshadowed by the announcement that founding bassist Steve Rippon was leaving the band, later admitting it was due to exhaustion from their punishing tour schedule.[12] He was replaced in the new year by Phil King.

*

While shoegaze seemed to be reaching its natural peak, the phenomenon had one last high water mark to leave behind. On November 11, 1991, after two and a half years of recording in nineteen different studios, My Bloody Valentine finally released their long-awaited follow-up to the genre-creating *Isn't Anything*: the genre-defining *Loveless*.

Alan McGee: *Loveless* was probably one of the hardest records I was ever involved in making. It cost about £270,000, which probably doesn't sound like that much, but in 1991, we were just a shoebox record company. Kevin had a method, and it took a long time, but it was such a good record that it was worth it.

And although My Bloody Valentine seemed to exist on another plane and had been largely absent from the shoegaze explosion, reviewers couldn't help but focus on their relationship to the scene.

Alan Moulder: It was quite strange how when we were making *Loveless*, this whole scene took off, and the Valentines seemed to get bigger and bigger and bigger without actually releasing anything. They became bigger in stature from all these other bands.

After calling out the Valentines' omnipresent influence on shoegaze and admitting that he was "hoping that this LP would shame the impostors back into oblivion," Simon Reynolds mused in *Melody Maker* that "*Loveless* isn't, quite, the record to do that. But it does reaffirm how unique, how peerless, MBV are."[13] Similarly, the *NME*'s Dele Fadele wrote, "Look beyond the instantly attractive 'sound-kaleidoscopes' of Curve, Chapterhouse, Slowdive and a hundred others and you'll see the blueprint that predates them," continuing, "*Loveless* fires a silver-coated bullet into the future, daring all-comers to try and recreate its mixture of moods, feelings, emotion, styles and, yes, innovations."[14]

Despite all the optimism that *Loveless* drew a road map for the future, the band's subsequent disappearance from releasing new music would suggest it was more akin to the end of the road—at least for the next twenty years or so.

Nathaniel Cramp: By the time they got to *Loveless*, they were so far on a different path that nothing could really follow that, which is why *they* couldn't follow it. All those bands were obviously inspired by their first album and those EPs going back to '88, but by the time *Loveless* came out, it was from another planet. It's a much more extreme, avant-garde sounding record. You can't really compare *Nowhere* or anything else to *Loveless*.

Paul Lester: *Loveless* was the culmination of it all. That was the epic, indulgent album that allegedly almost wrecked Creation Records, and there was almost nowhere to go after it. That ticket had been taken as far as it could go, so the only way to proceed from *Loveless* and shoegazing at that point was back toward more traditional songcraft.

Despite early signs of fatigue from the British music press, shoegaze closed out its golden year by reaching new shores— specifically in America, where the sound was really just catching on.

In a December piece for *The New York Times*, Simon Reynolds summarized the scene for US readers, writing, "This year, the most popular phenomenon in British alternative rock is a wave of hazy neo-psychedelic guitar groups."[15] While noting that "Some critics call them 'shoe-gazers' because of their on-stage bashfulness," Reynolds opted to call them "dream pop," before highlighting releases by My Bloody Valentine, Slowdive, Lush, Chapterhouse, Ride, and Swervedriver. The article ends on the promising note: " . . . with dance-rock groups like EMF and the Charlatans seeming like yesterday's news, dream pop is increasingly identifiable and saleable, and major labels are starting to pay attention."

Twelve months later, the forecast would look a little darker.

9 What's in a Name?

So let's talk about "shoegaze," and when and how the name came to be.

What we know beyond a reasonable doubt is that the word shoegaze—originally *shoegazing*—was coined by the late Andy Ross, a part-time *Sounds* writer and full-time head of Food Records, the label that subsequently launched Blur into the stratosphere. A regular fixture at Syndrome and in the Camden Town scene that became The Scene That Celebrates Itself, Ross was attending a Lush gig at the Venue in New Cross on March 15, 1991, where Blur were supporting alongside Moose, when he made the observation that famously shy Moose singer Russell Yates was looking at his feet the entire time. Veteran PR agent Polly Birkbeck, who was Ross' assistant at the time, remembers it well.

Polly Birkbeck: I was friends with Moose, Chapterhouse, and Lush, and I was always going about how great they were. Andy preferred bands who like to jump up and down on stage—shoegazing was the complete antithesis of that—so he made a joke about Moose looking at their shoes all the time. He called them "shoegazers," and we both thought that was a really funny word.

Funny enough, although "shoegazing" is generally understood to describe how shoegaze guitarists would stare at their effects pedals, Russell was in fact looking down at something else.

Moose McKillop: Andy Ross couldn't understand why Russell was just staring at his feet the whole time, but it wasn't a pedal selection issue. What he was doing was staring at the lyrics written on the floor. He just had no memory for lyrics, so he had sheets of A4 with the words.

Now here's where the story gets fuzzy. One popular·narrative is that Ross penned the word "shoegazing" in a live review of the show published in *Sounds*, but according to Polly—and backed up by Sonic Cathedral's Nathaniel Cramp, who has scoured every issue of *Sounds* from the period—the Moose review is a myth.

In a 2016 blog post for *The Huffington Post*, Ross himself shared his version of events.[1] After *Sounds* was abruptly sold and shuttered by its publisher in April 1991—along with its sister paper, *Record Mirror*—Ross no longer had an outlet to coin his latest musical musings. Thus, he pitched "shoegazing" to his influential friends, *NME* journalists Steve Lamacq and Simon Williams, over lunch at an Italian restaurant in Soho, which he dates to October 9, 1991.

Polly Birkbeck: Andy used to go out drinking with Steve Lamacq, and used ["shoegazing"] in conversation. Then Steve used it in a story about Slowdive.

Lamacq's news bulletin-style blurb reads:

> SLOWDIVE have announced details of a third EP and cluster of British dates. "Holding Our Breath" is released through Creation on June 3, and features three new tracks, "Catch The Breeze", "Shine", "Albatross", plus a cover of Syd Barrett's "Golden Hair". The hotly tipped **shoe-gazers** also play Manchester

Boardwalk (June 23), Sheffield University (24), Reading University (25), Salisbury Arts Centre (26), Northampton Irish Centre (27), London ULU (28). Oxford Venue (29), Birmingham Foundry (30).[2]

The only problem with Andy Ross' account: his timeline doesn't line up with that first appearance of "shoe-gazers," which was in the May 25, 1991, edition of *NME*. Sadly, Ross passed away in 2022, so we can't ask him to clarify, although the obvious explanation is that he got the dates wrong. But there's more.

Cramp's sleuthing also shakes the widely accepted notion that "shoegazing" came *after* Steve Sutherland's "The Scene That Celebrates Itself." While the prevailing timeline—enforced by various online histories of the movement, including the Wikipedia entry for "shoegaze" as of this writing—says that "The Scene" was coined in 1990, the earliest appearance, confirmed by Sutherland, is a live review of Moose published in *Melody Maker* on June 8, 1991. It reads:

MOOSE
CAMDEN UNDERWORLD, LONDON

There's Damon from Blur, Miki from Lush, Andrew from Chapterhouse, Mark from Ride, whatsit from the Manic Streets, even Pete Wylie . . . have the stars turned out to see Moose or what? Just lately there's been some snide criticism of **The Scene That Celebrates Itself**. Some folks are saying it's growing too incestuous, that such back-slapping support will lead to sycophancy, that honest appraisal will inevitably suffer and that, if they're not too careful, this bright young bunch will become too homogenous, too self-satisfied with preening to the converted. Some folks are too f***ing cynical for their own good. If anything binds together The Scene That Celebrates Itself it's that it revels in its differences. Ride can admonish Chapterhouse for making "Pearl" too baggy, Blur can flaunt their sudden success, everyone can mock the Manic Streets. The only thing this bunch have in common apart from a life-enhancing enthusiasm for music that simultaneously pushes further into the wastelands of your psyche while scampering higher up the charts is that they all loathe Curve. Oh, and I guess they all wish they sounded like Moose.[3]

So, despite "shoegazing" predating it by a couple of weeks, "The Scene That Celebrates Itself" seems to have caught on first and lived a short life as the dominant term. And while nobody liked "The Scene" label, "shoegaze" tended to be even more hated by the bands it described.

Emma Anderson: The word "shoegaze" is not a term of endearment. It was a piss take.

Miki Berenyi: "The Scene That Celebrates Itself" came and went within two months, because then "shoegaze" took over. Andy Ross meant it like, *Look at these shit bands who stare at their pedals and hide behind their fringes. They're all really boring and I can't tell one from the other.* It was not a lovely term that anyone wanted to be a part of.

David Quantick: It wasn't terrifically insulting, but it basically created this great image of not just the shoes, but the hair over their eyes, bent over their guitars, not engaging with the audience.

Paul Lester: All bands hate labels, but with shoegaze, the sense of derision was factored into the name from the word go.

Chris Roberts: It was a throwaway comment in the pub. There's no way anyone thought it would've stuck. It's such a lame name, and it doesn't even work as an umbrella term. I mean, loads of bands from other genres look at their feet. Pink Floyd stared at their shoes. Does that make them shoegaze?

Greg Ackell: One could argue that the Cure or the Jesus and Mary Chain were also pretty fucking still on stage. The Velvet Underground had that kind of stoic, backlit presence. It's weird to me that that would be an assail, because I think it's a cool look.

Adam Franklin: It's a genre named after a footwear item. It was derogatory in the same way that "Krautrock" was coined by an Englishman thirty years after the end of the Second World War, but then it stuck.

Greg Ackell: There's a great line in the Whit Stillman movie *The Last Days of Disco* where they're walking out of the proverbial Studio 54, and somebody calls someone a yuppie, and the guy that gets called the yuppie goes, "Do yuppies even exist? No one says, 'I am a yuppie.' It's always the other guy who's a yuppie. I think for a group to exist, somebody has to admit to being part of it." And shoegazing was a bit like that. It's only something you would call somebody, not something anyone would call themselves.

10 Shoegaze Fading

In 1992, popular currents were shifting in the UK, and the tides of shoegaze were beginning to recede.

Moose McKillop: There was a certain feeling of diminishing returns. You go from playing ULU for a thousand people, to two years later playing for 350 people, and then 250 . . . And you realize there's a certain direction that this is going in.

Whether this trend was instigated by the influential press or the music-listening public, for someone like Steve Sutherland, who made the jump from deputy editor at *Melody Maker* to editor of *NME* that year, it was a bit like reading tea leaves.

Steve Sutherland: Ultimately my job as an editor was to sell papers, because if you don't sell papers, then you don't exist. So you're always watching what your readership appears to tell you it wants, but at the same time you're trying to inspire them to listen to something else. It's a weird dynamic.

Chris Roberts: People get bored with praising the same thing for a few months. It always had to be the hot new thing. The editors would perhaps assume or decide that, *Oh, the public are bored with shoegaze now*, whether they were or weren't.

For anyone who had followed the British music press before shoegaze, the flight path was fairly predictable.

Miki Berenyi: Looking back, I think the pattern was that they would find the next big thing and talk about them constantly, so that people keep buying the magazine. Then, when everyone gets sick of them, they'd start kicking the shit out of them, because that's entertaining as well. Readers love it.

Sonic Boom: It still happens occasionally, where they come and stay at your house and be your best friend, and then they go away and dump on you in the piece, trying to be a real smart ass. *NME* were the worst for it. I always summed it up by saying a really good day for them was when they'd done an interview with a band and then the band broke up. *And it happened.*

Stephen Patman: I think the initial interest in our bands was genuine, like, *These guys could go somewhere. I wanna attach myself to this.* Then when it didn't go anywhere, they all ran a mile away and didn't wanna be associated with us.

David Quantick: When you have a relationship with a band, it can be a bit like dumping somebody you don't want to marry. You start off with a band, they get early coverage, journalists come to see them playing pubs, they get a deal with 4AD or Creation, the singles come out, they get rave reviews, the album comes out and it's pretty good, except the cracks start to appear. The second album comes out, and they're tired. And you think, *Well, Slowdive aren't gonna be around in a year. They haven't got the stamina.*

Rachel Goswell: It was all very complimentary at the beginning, but that's what they would do: they would pick up certain bands, throw loads of accolades at them, and then a little way down the line came the backlash. The actual working title of the third Slowdive EP was *Holding Our Breath Waiting for the Backlash*, because we knew it was coming. It was inevitable.

David Quantick: "Build it up and knock them down," we often used to say.

Steve Sutherland: If you got eighteen months, you were very lucky.

Part of this mounting backlash was wrapped up in a largely unfounded perception that the musicians of shoegaze came from privileged middle-class backgrounds, which is a real dig in class-obsessed England.

Chris Roberts: There's an inverted snobbery in the British music press where they don't want posh middle-class musicians doing well—they want working-class, rootsy, honest grafting types to do well. It's almost absurd because you can get great art from anywhere, but because these bands were long-haired hippie types who smoked pot, they were typecast as privileged or entitled, which was so far from the truth.

Neil Halstead: At that time there was definitely a big North-South divide between the Manchester scene and the London scene, and we were seen as Southern softies whose parents had bought us our guitars. It was crazy because the same journalists would be all over Dinosaur Jr. or the Lemonheads, not mentioning the fact that they came from quite wealthy backgrounds, and in the same issue we'd be getting all this attitude.

Miki Berenyi: Meanwhile you'll get someone who's quite privileged and well-off, who will just put on a cockney accent and act like they're some fucking chimney sweep. Blur was middle class, whatever they wanted to tell the public. I am an outsider to the British class system, so I've never particularly understood why you wouldn't just say what the fuck your background is.

Nathaniel Cramp: The truth of the matter is that a lot of music journalists who were working at *NME* were posh and middle class themselves. When I was there, there were loads of people that were from Oxford University and places like that, so it's almost like a weird self-loathing thing where they fetishized a working-class band like Oasis over people that were more like themselves.

Baseless or not, the press' response to this perception was to play it up and mock it mercilessly. The ultimate example of this lampoonery was a short-lived column in the *NME* titled "Memoirs of a Shoegazing Gentleman," penned between October 1991 and February 1992 by music critic and aspiring comedy writer David Quantick. Told from the fictional perspective of an upper-class caricature named Lord Tarquin, the ridiculous diary-like entries detail the irreverent escapades and gossip of an elite boarding school that all the shoegaze bands supposedly attended.

The first such column began:

What ho old things! Just popped back from a round of fives in the Lower Quad with Russell from Moose! Top-hole shuffle! Russell was ten up on a double shubunkin when he dropped the bally spinnaker! The cream buns are on him next time we pop into Mrs Shoggins' tea shop in the village!

It's been a whizzo week for my Lordship! Woke up with a dead bird in my bed which had been put there by new bug Russell from Chapterhouse—but I got my own back by "sneaking" him to the house master for bashing the bishop over some girlie magazines! Haw haw! Russell tried to get me back by making me an apple pie bed, which is a crumbly old wheeze and three bags full!

After kedgeree it was double Latin and Miki and Emma from Lush absolutely bished up the subjunctive of "richo" and had to stay behind and have their Buntys confiscated. MIDDLE CLASS OR WHAT?![1]

David Quantick: There was no information in it, and I clearly have no idea what shoegaze is. The band names were correct, but the names of the members were by and large wrong. There was no mention of the music in any way, and by a certain point I just was trying to think of euphemisms for masturbation. "Buffing the happy lamp" was the one I remember.

Emma Anderson: That was brilliant. He made it sound like we were all at private school together, living in dormitories, speaking in Latin, and dressed in tunics. It was actually quite funny, but there was an element of ridicule.

Chris Roberts: It was just total fantasy on David's part, but it kind of stuck a bit, and that irritated the bands.

David Quantick: It's solely based on this entirely made-up idea that all the shoegazing bands went to exclusive private schools, of which there is no evidence for. I think there was a genuine belief at the beginning that there was something middle class about the music. I can't really say why, but it wasn't party music, let's say that.

Steve Sutherland: It was easy to take the piss out of them, but it's easy to take the piss out of everybody, isn't it? Every music paper had a satirical part, and we used to rip the piss out of the goths, the grunge guys, Britpop—everybody got their turn. If they were a UK band, they'd all grown up reading the music press, so they knew the game.

*

Despite the sense that sound had run its course and The Scene had splintered, some of shoegaze's best albums were released between 1992 and 1993, with early bands maturing and newer entrants offering new iterations of the noise-melody paradigm. Still, with "shoegaze" now firmly established as a vulnerability, even positive reviews of new music used the association as a point of criticism.

In January 1992, 4AD finally released Lush's sublime Robin Guthrie-produced full-length, *Spooky*, which you could call their first, second, or third album, depending on whether you count mini-album *Scar* or their US/Japan-only compilation, *Gala*. In her lukewarm review for *NME*, critic Betty Page seemed to openly fight her waning patience with the shoegaze sound.[2] "After a good run of press encouragement as luxuriant as their name, it seems Lush are now due for a good kicking," she wrote, before patronizing them as an "easy, soft, succulent target" for words like "Shoey, fey, wistful, eth*r*al," and complaining about the buried vocals ("But, oh, how I wish you could hear the words"). Page concluded that while *Spooky* has something to offer beneath the surface, and though "it seems accepted that Lush are great people . . . they're yet to make great music."

A week later Creation dropped the Boo Radleys' album *Everything's Alright Forever*, which fused shoegaze guitar fuzz with Teenage Fanclub power pop. Calling the album a "masterpiece," the *NME*'s Keith Cameron commended the band's prideful, not-so-shoegazey attitude, writing how "stout-hearted self-opinion was a cheering presence in 1991's (complacen)sea of mumbles."[3]

Still flying high above the rest, Ride distanced themselves from the movement on their tour de force sophomore LP, *Going Blank Again*, explicitly so on the eight-minute opener, "Leave Them All Behind."

Mark Gardener: There was a whole crop of short-named, noisy bands suddenly coming out everywhere. I was a bit deluded, but it felt a bit like everyone was trying to do what we were doing and steal our thunder, so it was a statement, like, *We will leave them all behind, because they're just not that great.*

While the rest of the album has enough shoegaze elements to be considered the genre classic it is, it also shows the band expanding their palette considerably.

Alan Moulder: They got more '60s sounding on *Going Blank Again*. I think you could see that a song like "Twisterella" isn't really shoegaze.

Steve Queralt: I felt like we were no longer a shoegaze band. Bands like R.E.M. and Massive Attack started to become influences, so we started using keyboards, strings, and Hammond organs. It wasn't like, *Oh no, we can't do that because it isn't noisy or indie enough.*

March marked two other seminal albums from part-time shoegazers: Curve's potent debut LP, *Doppelgänger*, which John Lydon (a.k.a. Johnny Rotten) called "the best thing he's heard in ages,"[4] and Pale Saints' immaculate second LP, *In Ribbons*, after which Ian Masters would leave the band due to creative differences.

Ian Masters: I almost left before *In Ribbons* was recorded because the atmosphere in the band was starting to go sour. Graham and Chris wanted to become a more mainstream rock band, and I wanted to keep going down the experimental route.

Although they would record a final album in 1994, with former Lush singer Meriel Barham assuming full-time lead vocal duties, it wasn't really Pale Saints, and it definitely wasn't shoegaze.

That spring, Creation introduced their latest shoegaze act, Adorable, with the release of their debut single, "Sunshine Smile," which got *Melody Maker*'s "Single of the Week" and subsequently topped the Indie Chart. Although Adorable's relevance would be short-lived—due in part to the members' prickly personalities—they would continue to release Top 5 singles throughout the year, leading up to their stellar 1993 full-length, *Against Perfection*, which remains a forgotten gem of the genre.

Around the same time, Blur released the non-album single "Popscene" into the world. Following the muted reception to their 1991 debut album, *Leisure*, the band opted to shed the guitar distortion in favor of more upbeat melodies, ska-inspired horns, and lyrics that bitched at the homogenous sound of the music industry. Though the release was dismissed by the press at the time, observers would later call it the first siren of Britpop. Tellingly, in an interview with the *NME*, Blur frontman Damon Albarn dissociated his band from the anti-fame shoegazers by openly admitting their commercial ambitions, saying, "I'd love 'Popscene' to be a big hit . . . But then again, there's a noisy indie group on [*Top of the Pops*] every week now. All looking very satisfied with their Number 18 . . ."[5]

A month later, *Melody Maker* made the bold move of putting an unknown group named Suede on their front cover, announcing them as "The Best New Band in Britain."[6] Released two weeks later, their debut single, "The Drowners," was anything but shoegaze, sounding more like the British glam rock of the '70s. Though the song would barely crack the Top 50 of the UK Singles Chart, Suede's debut album one year later would mark the true start of the Britpop era. But for the time being they represented an interesting new blip on the constantly cycling indie rock radar.

Interestingly, that March also introduced "All in the Mind," the debut single from future Britpoppers the Verve. While the genre's stylistic constraints couldn't contain the rockstar charisma of frontman Richard Ashcroft for long, the band's early psychedelic space rock was certifiably shoegazey all the way through to their 1993 LP, *A Storm in Heaven*.

While the bubble maintained by the British music press was becoming increasingly hostile to the shoegaze scene, the bands found safe harbor across the Atlantic, where the sound had more room to roam.

Stephen Patman: One thing we noticed was that people in the States didn't give a shit about what the music press in the UK were saying. They were just listening to the music and saying, "You guys are great! I love your album!" Whereas the UK public were reading the music press and going, "It must be shit, 'cause they're saying it's shit."

Christian Savill: Even when we were having a shit time in the UK, because the music press were being absolutely vile, we'd go to America and it'd be really nice. Everyone would just listen to us with an open mind and take it for what it is.

Naturally, it was only a matter of time before America started producing its own shoegaze bands. One of the first to emerge, and probably the most accepted in the UK scene, was Drop Nineteens. Formed in the dorm rooms of Boston University circa 1990, the band centered around vocalist and guitarist Greg Ackell, plus bassist Steve Zimmerman, guitarist Motohiro Yasue, drummer Chris Roof, and vocalist-guitarist Paula Kelley. Like many American indie kids, Ackell and his cohorts religiously read imported copies of *NME* and *Melody Maker*, and thus had their tastes formed around the same bands as their contemporaries from London and the Thames Valley.

Greg Ackell: Drop Nineteens wouldn't exist without [Spacemen 3's] *The Perfect Prescription*, [My Bloody Valentine's]

Isn't Anything, and [Sonic Youth's] *Daydream Nation*. "All I Need" from *Isn't Anything* was the sexiest, coolest fucking sound I had ever heard. There's just something so interesting about the noise and the distortion.

When the group started writing and recording around those common influences in 1991, they managed to stumble upon the shoegaze sound without even knowing the full scope of what was already happening across the pond.

Greg Ackell: We had done these demos that were pretty derivative of My Bloody Valentine and Cocteau Twins, but at the time we weren't really aware of shoegaze. We were aware of the name Slowdive, but we hadn't really heard their music. When I saw them described in *Melody Maker*, which you used to be able to get at Newbury Comics, it was like, *Wow, that sounds like us.*

Rather than trying to get gigs around Boston, Ackell printed up cassettes of their eight-track demo and mailed them out to every label in his record collection, many of which were in England.

Greg Ackell: I had zero expectations for it. Zero. But within a week and a half I was getting calls from those labels. We got so many calls that it behooved me to go to London. So the band chipped in and got me a plane ticket.

After a whirlwind tour meeting with various London indies, befriending Andy and Stephen from Chapterhouse, and experiencing The Scene That Celebrates Itself, Ackell flew back home. Unbeknownst to him, a woman who worked at 4AD had sent their demo cassette to *Melody Maker* and *NME*.

Greg Ackell: I got back to Boston, and a week later I got a call from one of the labels saying, "You're Single of the Week in *Melody Maker*." I was like, "What do you mean? There is no single. We're still unsigned. We've never played live before."

"Funny old world," observed Simon Williams in the *NME* review of the demos. "One minute those Beatles and Stones boys are ripping (off) their way through the Encyclopedia of American R&B, the next Boston's Drop Nineteens are joyriding through Britain's Home Counties and performing impeccable handbrake turns in the drives of the palatial mansions belonging to Slowhouse and Chapterdive."[7]

Eventually, the band signed with Hut in the UK and released their seminal debut album, *Delaware*, in June 1992. In a review that managed to skillfully praise Drop Nineteens while denigrating their UK counterparts, *Melody Maker's* Everett True wrote,

> Remember "The Scene"? It's of no great credit to my colleagues and the British "indie" labels that at last we have a band with The Scene aesthetic who justify all the ridiculous plaudits . . . How ironic then, that the first decent album in a Scene style should show up from America (Boston, to be precise), so late in the day.[8]

Just behind *Delaware*, the American shoegaze parade continued that autumn with the excellent debut albums of Washington, DC, shoegazers Lilys (*In the Presence of Nothing*) and Los Angeles shoegazers Medicine (*Shot Forth Self Living*), followed in early 1993 by fellow Boston band Swirlies (*Blonder Tongue Audio Baton*).

Outside of the exciting new American bands, noteworthy shoegaze releases slowed in the latter half of '92. While a bit too groovy and straightforward for true shoegaze, Th' Faith Healers' rollicking debut, *Lido*, is a euphoric twist on the sound. Similarly, Kitchens of Distinction's still shoegazey third LP, *The Death of Cool*, has been called their best by fans, despite selling half as many copies as *Strange Free World*.

Though Catherine Wheel didn't interact much with the scene, being from the Norfolk seaside town of Great Yarmouth, one album that definitely checked all the shoegaze boxes is the band's first full-length, *Ferment*, which, like Swervedriver at their most psychedelic, adds heavy guitar riffs to the genre's swirling, smoke-filled atmospheres.

Labeling Catherine Wheel "the black sheep of the shoegaze family," *Pitchfork*'s Ben Cardew retrospectively called half the songs on *Ferment* "enduring shoegaze-disco classics, while 'Black Metallic,' in its full seven-minute glory, makes a strong claim to being the genre's 'Stairway to Heaven.'"[9]

Given the fact that their name comes from a medieval torture device, not to mention lead singer Rob Dickinson being the cousin of Iron Maiden's Bruce Dickinson, it isn't shocking that the band dropped the psychedelia in favor of a harder, more metal-leaning shoegaze sound on 1993's *Chrome*, after which they evolved into a straight hard rock band.

After arriving late on the scene, releasing a thrilling trio of 1991 EPs (*Jack*, *Cool Breeze*, *Reprise*), and playing highly touted live gigs with seemingly every other band mentioned in this book, by the time Moose finally released their debut album, they were somehow the first to decisively move beyond the shoegaze sound. Released in September 1992, *...XYZ* saw the band ditching their noisy roots for country and western-tinged balladry and a Harry Nilsson cover. In a perverted act of promotional generosity, *Melody Maker* ran a bizarre three-page spread seemingly designed to distance Moose from the scene whose two names they were responsible for inspiring, while also dancing on its grave.[10]

Paul Lester: I remember being commissioned by the editor of *Melody Maker* in 1992 to write a *where-are-they-now* type article titled "Whatever Happened to Shoegazing?" which just sounds incredible now. It's like it was ancient history, but it was only a year before. That's how fast moving the British scene was then.

In the profoundly tongue-in-cheek piece, which also gathered some opinions from Slowdive's Neil Halstead, Blur's Damon Albarn, and the Telescopes' Stephen Lawrie, Paul Lester briefly summarizes the scene's supposed rise and fall before an interview where Moose appears to shit-talk various shoegaze bands.

Moose McKillop: It was supposed to be an interview about our album, but we got asked about a bunch of bands we knew right at the end, and that turned out to be the only bit they used. The selective quotes barely mention all the nice things we said. Typical of the music press at the time.

While the backbiting feature's intentions were all in good fun, the underlying message was clear: shoegaze was dead.

Paul Lester: It was brutal. It was cruel. We were praising these guys to the hilt in '91 like they were the future of everything, and then by '92 we'd dismissed them as relics of the past.

11 Shoegaze Falls Off a Cliff

By 1993, popular interest in shoegaze had almost entirely evaporated, leaving the movement dying on the cross as far as the public was concerned.

Jane Savidge: Most movements peter out and end up eating themselves. Shoegazing didn't do that. Shoegazing fell off a cliff.

Stephen Patman: It was just quashed by these two monoliths that were taking off. You had grunge, which was a lot of mediocre bands riding on the coattails of Nirvana, and then you had Britpop, which really hooked into the political climate at the time. There was a euphoria about a change in politics alongside the rise of this supposedly rebellious music into the mainstream. The whole landscape changed, and we got buried under it.

Chris Roberts: I think that its life span as a hot topic was probably just about right, because where could it really have gone? It was starting to get a little bit repetitious on the second and third albums.

Steve Sutherland: There was a sense that all of them had done the best thing they were gonna do. Everybody knows that the first Ride album was better than the second Ride album, which was way better than the third Ride album. Same thing with Lush. Although decent records were made, the excitement around the scene had just burned itself out. And so the next thing moved in quite quickly.

Jane Savidge: The thing about movements is that it's a two-edged sword. If you had a band that you couldn't align with a movement, there was often no reason for a magazine to write about them over the 400 other bands out there, so a lot of these bands might not have gone anywhere if they hadn't been part of the movement. But the other edge of the sword is that when the movement dies, the band dies with it.

You might say the death knell tolled on March 29, 1993—the day Suede's self-titled debut hit record shops across the UK. Since the *Melody Maker* cover that dubbed them "The Best New Band in Britain" a year earlier, the band had dropped a trio of increasingly hyped singles—"The Drowners," "Metal Mickey," and "Animal Nitrate"—and appeared on eighteen additional magazine and newspaper covers. As a result, *Suede* was an instant hit, topping the charts with enough force to become the fastest-selling UK debut of any band up to that point.

Hitting back at the grunge that had ruled the press for the past year and a half, the April issue of *Select* magazine would formally introduce the Britpop era with the famous "Yanks Go Home!" cover, on which Suede frontman Brett Anderson poses sensually in front of the Union Jack.[1]

Polly Birkbeck: Suede and Britpop just swept everything else aside.

Steve Sutherland: Suede kind of killed shoegaze, because they looked like they could be shoegazers, but they behaved like traditional rock stars. The way they came out, they seemed fully formed, and you'd have to be a complete fool not to see that they were gonna be massive for a while, so you needed to be on board.

Released six weeks later, Blur's second album, *Modern Life Is Rubbish*, reinvented the group in a similar image. While it wasn't the smash hit that *Suede* was, their next album, 1994's *Parklife*, would elevate them to one of the movement's "big four," alongside Suede, Pulp, and Oasis.

Meanwhile, shoegaze had been relegated to a punching bag for the music press. While everyone had their turn, a few bands were favorite targets.

Adam Franklin: There was an element of bullying with the press coverage of shoegaze, and certain bands took the brunt a lot more. I think Chapterhouse probably took the largest brunt of it.

Steve Queralt: We [in Ride] never really got any bad press. We might have gotten a few average reviews for our third and fourth albums, but we never got slated or ridiculed like what Slowdive went through. They got treated *really* badly.

Rachel Goswell: I always said that the journalists at *NME* and *Melody Maker* were failed musicians who take their bitterness out on certain bands, and we were one of them.

Stephen Patman: Slowdive was like Satan's spawn in the music press. I remember when the Manic Street Preachers said in an interview, "I don't wanna meet Slowdive, 'cuz they're worse than Hitler." [Technically, Richey Edwards said, "I will always hate Slowdive more than Hitler."]

Chris Roberts: It got a bit nasty at times. I mean, you're hitting on these indie bands who are just trying to do their thing, not superstar millionaires like Bono, who deserves a bit of satirizing.

Christian Savill: It's amazing just how they could just say, *Oh, actually this band's shit now*, and people would stop coming to your gigs. When you're young like we were, it's hard to take.

Andy Sherriff: It probably did affect your mental health being pilloried in public. It was like being bullied.

Neil Halstead: We all got a bit of a mauling, to be honest. Slowdive, Chapterhouse, Moose, Pale Saints—everyone got a good kicking. They really didn't hold back.

There is perhaps no greater example of how the shoegaze bands were skewered than with Slowdive's second album, *Souvlaki*, released on June 1, 1993. The album, which thirty years later is considered one of shoegaze's crowning achievements—ranking behind only *Loveless* on *Pitchfork*'s list—was a backbreaking and heartbreaking effort for the quintet, who had to write and record it while navigating the fact that Neil and Rachel, who had been romantically involved since the band took off, had broken up.

Unimpressed by that story, the album's inherent beauty, or even the fact that Brian Eno helped record a couple tracks, *Souvlaki* was panned beyond recognition by *Melody Maker*'s

Dave Simpson, who famously declared, "I would rather drown choking in a bath full of porridge than ever listen to it again."

Nathaniel Cramp: I mean, that's quite extreme. That level of hatred is very strange for bands that don't really provoke that kind of feeling.

Simon Scott: By the time *Souvlaki* came out, they didn't even give it a chance. I don't think they even fucking listened.

Alan Moulder: I had a hit list of numerous journalists that I wanted to take down. Emotionally, you spend ages on things, you're very passionate about it, and then somebody just dismisses it and completely misses the point. And you can feel that their angle isn't totally based on music. It's based on their paper's policy. There were a lot of feelings of injustice.

Meanwhile, the bands who were less targeted were often simply relegated to the back burner of critical attention. The pop-leaning Ride and Lush managed to stay afloat by distancing themselves from the scene. Swervedriver—whose fast and furious 1993 album, *Mezcal Head*, got an eight out of ten in *NME* and has since been hailed as "the lost classic of the shoegaze movement"[2]—was blessed by the fact that (1) many people felt they never should have been put into the shoegaze scene in the first place, and (2) that their sound allowed them to be more successful in America, where they toured with the likes of Soundgarden and the Smashing Pumpkins.

With shoegaze essentially exiled as the genre non grata, the original bands had little choice but to evolve if they wanted to survive. Whether or not it was a conscious act to pivot their sounds, they all did. After spreading their wings on *Going Blank Again*, Ride left shoegaze entirely behind on the '60s folk rock homage, *Carnival of Light* (1994). Lush grew increasingly less fuzzy on 1994's *Split* before giving their best rendition of Britpop on 1996s *Lovelife*. Having already flirted with the baggy sound of Madchester on their earlier records, Chapterhouse turned in an electronic dance record with 1993s *Blood Music*. In their own way, even Swervedriver minimized their American references to emulate the en vogue sounds of Britain on 1995s *Ejector Seat Reservation*, which earned them strong reviews in the UK but lost them the support of their US label.

Loz Colbert: We believed in what we were doing, but some of the influences were just too diluted and out of reach for us to fully grasp. It didn't make sense to who we were, and the cake didn't fully bake.

Andy Bell: I think if Ride had one real failing, it was that we left that sound behind too soon.

Miki Berenyi: Back with the Cocteau Twins and the Pixies, you could be a huge indie band and attract massive crowds of people, but now it was all measured by chart positions, and if you didn't get in the charts, you could fuck off. So we wrote *Lovelife*.

Emma Anderson: By then we weren't really doing shoegaze anymore.

Andy Sherriff: I got more into dance music, and Stephen had got more into '70s rock. Some of it works and some of it doesn't.

Jimmy Hartridge: That was a funny album. You can hear the Britpop crossing with the noisy shoegaze sound. That photo on the inner sleeve, where we're all sitting in the cafe, was the sort of thing Blur would've done.

It's worth noting that, with the exception of Boo Radleys—who went full Britpop with their irritatingly chipper 1995 radio hit "Wake Up Boo!"—none of these albums succeeded in maintaining the former shoegazers' commercial or critical standing, let alone elevating them to a higher echelon of pop relevance (with the possible exception of Lush). Meanwhile, rather than adapt to popular trends, Slowdive found a way to become even less commercially viable with the electronic post-rock experiment of 1995's *Pygmalion*, while My Bloody Valentine simply went into hibernation for two decades, despite signing to Island Records in October 1992 for a reported £250,000.

Nick Chaplin: I think bands like Lush, and to a lesser extent, Chapterhouse and Ride, did try and push it a little bit more commercially. We ended up going in the other direction with *Pygmalion*.

Neil Halstead: I wasn't into the guitar thing anymore. I was much more into electronic music—from LFO and Aphex Twin to Ryuichi Sakamoto to John Cage—so I ended up pulling the band in that direction.

Paul Lester: My Bloody Valentine did *Isn't Anything* and *Loveless*, and then went quiet for twenty years. So their response to *What do we do now?* was to do nothing.

*

Over the next few years, each of the original bands would break up. Chapterhouse was the first to go, though not for the interpersonal reasons bands typically split up for.

Stephen Patman: We released *Blood Music* into a music press that had already decided they weren't gonna like it. We had journalists like Dele Fadele, who was a big fan and wanted to review it for the *NME*, but the editor wouldn't let him because it was paper policy not to like us.

With the album doomed to fail in their home country, their labels felt the album had a better chance in the States. Having moved to Arista Records in America, the album even had the enthusiasm of music mogul Clive Davis as they embarked on a US tour. Shit hit the fan, however, when they became entangled in a convoluted legal battle between Killing Joke bassist Martin "Youth" Glover and Alex Patterson of electronic duo the Orb.

Stephen Patman: We'd done an instrumental on *Blood Music* that featured spoken word poetry by a friend of Youth, who had set up WAU! Mr. Modo Recordings with Alex Patterson. As the label grew, they started to argue over who owned it. As it turned out, this poet took Alex's side of the argument and thought he was getting back at Youth by suing us for using his lyrics on our album. So halfway through the American tour, we got an affidavit saying to stop selling this record.

Rather than withdrawing *Blood Music* from stores, Chapterhouse's labels agreed to stop manufacturing or promoting the album, leaving the band two albums into a five-album deal and owing the label a ton of money for their unrecouped advance.

Andy Sherriff: When you have a major record deal, the record company has to take up the option for you to get paid the next advance, but they can decide not to take that option until you produce something they want. You can't take your stuff to another label because that's breaking your contract, so you end up in this catch-22 situation.

Stephen Patman: We started writing again, but it was never gonna be commercial enough for them to make their money back. It was all about Blur and Oasis at the time, and we weren't gonna compete with that, so in '94 or '95, after a year of demoing, we decided to quit.

*

When Nirvana's Kurt Cobain died by suicide on April 5, 1994, many were quick to say that grunge died with him. Six days later, on April 11, Creation Records released "Supersonic," the debut single from Oasis, completing Britpop's ascent to total dominance.

Adam Franklin: I remember coming back from the Smashing Pumpkins tour in 1994. When we left it was still long hair and plaid shirts, and the tail end of grunge. We came back to London six weeks later and everyone's wearing Adidas and tight '70s T-shirts with cropped, spiky peroxide hair. It was a vastly different scene, and in the meantime, all the shoegaze bands disappeared overnight.

Sounding at times like a '90s redux of T. Rex, the Sex Pistols, and the Kinks, Britpop—a name suggested by *Select* journalist and future *BBC Radio 6 Music* host Stuart Maconie—was a bright, catchy, and explicitly British response to the American angst of grunge and the shy, introverted haze of shoegaze. The public ate it up like they hadn't heard real pop music in years.

Nathaniel Cramp: When Kurt Cobain died, Britpop was already looming, like an antidote to the perceived misery of grunge.

Jane Savidge: Grunge and shoegaze were about some dismal things. Britpop was about exciting, glamorous, and peculiarly British things.

Alan McGee: Damon Albarn, Noel Gallagher, and Jarvis Cocker were just such great songwriters. It was a great time for young British rock and roll bands with great fucking songs that could actually break through.

Just as important as the sound, however, was the fact that Britpop was a tabloid circus of epic proportions, with sex, drugs, conflict, giant rock star personalities, and bona fide hits. In other words, it was all the things shoegaze wasn't.

David Quantick: Britpop was extroverted. It was about cocaine, getting drunk, shouting, bright colors, and easy-to-understand imagery, whereas shoegaze was introverted, mysterious, and inarticulate.

Neil Halstead: The press wanted more conflicts. They wanted bands to hate each other, and they wanted good quotes, which obviously Britpop provided. We just weren't exciting enough.

Nathaniel Cramp: The music papers were always looking for someone who was gonna be massive. Steve Sutherland, who was editor of *NME* for the "Battle of Britpop" cover, desperately wanted a band that he could attach the paper to that was gonna be massive. He'd really hyped up Ride and Chapterhouse, but that concept of record sales being the maker of whether a band is good or not was an alien concept to indie bands.

Steve Sutherland: We tried to make it pop music, and it was anti-pop. I can remember articles about Lush saying they could be the new ABBA: they had two boys and two girls, the music was kind of cute, and you had Miki and Emma, who looked great. And then we had Ride, who were really good-looking boys—they could be pin-ups. But none of them were imbued with that Damon Albarn drive, that *want* to be famous.

Andy Sherriff: In retrospect, that was quite a toxic time. It was quite aggressive and misogynistic, and it was all about success.

Miki Berenyi: There was always sexism around, but with Britpop, it was celebrated.

David Quantick: Britpop was horrific. There were some good bands, but the whole Britpop theme was basically someone on a Union Jack guitar playing a crappy version of "Waterloo Sunset" while shouting in a cockney accent.

Chris Roberts: It seemed like the only criteria was whether you were commercially successful. It was like these new bands didn't care about being good, so much as *Have you got a hit?* So the goal posts were moved, and it became a bit more cynical. When Britpop became commercially successful and crossed over into the national press and TV, it dwarfed any impact that shoegaze had. It blew everything else to dust.

Inside Creation Records—the bona fide nerve center of shoegaze—the arrival of Oasis had its own implications.

Andy Bell: Oasis came along in '93, and I was a huge fan. I personally went to see them ten or fifteen times during those first few years, and I loved the band. It was really, really big for Creation because they were the biggest thing that happened to that label.

Chris Roberts: I don't think anyone expected Britpop to balloon as huge as it did, apart from savvy businessmen like Alan McGee, who switched from saying, "My Bloody Valentine are the best band in the world" to saying, "Oasis are the best" in the space of a few years.

Alan McGee: When Oasis started selling 23 million records, things changed for Creation. We were cash rich, and I was suddenly a genius. But I suppose I probably lost contact with a lot of music.

By 1995, when the band's second album, *(What's the Story) Morning Glory?*, was shattering records and taking over the world, Creation simply had no use for most of its roster anymore, dropping Slowdive and Swervedriver in quick succession.

Nick Chaplin: Creation entirely threw their weight behind Oasis, to the detriment of everybody else on the label, other than maybe Primal Scream. They were getting Top 10 singles with Primal Scream and Oasis, so by the mid-'90s, we knew it was over.

Jimmy Hartridge: Creation signed Oasis and dropped us in the same timeframe, because if you've got a band that's gonna sell 30 million copies, who's gonna keep a band that's gonna sell a few thousand? What's the point?

Miki Berenyi: That environment was all about signing up bands for a load of money, throwing shit against the wall, and if it didn't stick, they were sacked off, whereas the bands in the shoegaze era were on independent labels that nurtured them. That whole independent ethic had gone.

Andy Sherriff: Indie music kind of died with Britpop and had to reinvent itself.

*

One after another, the remaining bands fizzled out, beginning with the beleaguered Slowdive. After the abysmal reception of *Souvlaki*, drummer Simon Scott jumped ship before they hit the iceberg.

Simon Scott: I got really frustrated with the band, so I just left. *Souvlaki* was doing badly, and there was some confusion with America, and the tour funding got pulled, so it felt like the band wasn't going anywhere.

While the rest of Slowdive stuck around for *Pygmalion*, the writing was on the wall.

Nick Chaplin: *Pygmalion* was so obscure compared to what came before. It was basically a Neil Halstead solo record. The rest of us did play on it, but it was very much like, "Oh, Nick, can you play a tiny bit of bass on this one song?" And then it gets looped.

Neil Halstead: It ended up not really being a band record. I think that pulled the band apart far more than me and Rachel splitting up on *Souvlaki*.

Rachel Goswell: The band was very dissipated by that point. Financially, we'd run out of money. I remember being present in the studio but not doing a lot. Nick and Christian were very negative and angry all the time, while Neil just wanted to finish the record.

Neil Halstead: Creation hadn't heard it until we finished the record. I think they got a massive shock when we played it for them. Alan McGee had told us early on that he'd wanted a pop record from us. They were like, *What is this?*

Rachel Goswell: By that point, McGee wasn't really there either. He was in rehab or busy with Oasis. He actually asked Neil whether Oasis could support us, but Neil was like, "No, I don't want them supporting us."

Alan McGee: By the time *Pygmalion* came out, Britpop was at full-fucking-blast, Blur and Oasis were heading toward being the biggest bands in the world, and there's Neil and Rachel putting out what was basically an ambient album. The timing of that record was terrible for the culture.

Neil Halstead: *Just for a Day* got awful reviews. *Souvlaki* got really bad reviews. *Pygmalion* just got very, very confused reviews.

Rachel Goswell: Creation dropped us about a week after the record came out. Tour canceled. We were expecting it. I'm not even sure there was a conversation about dissolving Slowdive. In the year since we'd finished the record, Neil had already been recording the stuff that became the first Mojave 3 album. Nick and Christian made it very clear they weren't interested in doing anything, so Neil and I just carried on.

*

After the classic rock misstep that was *Carnival of Light*, Ride was knocked off their throne and flailing.

Loz Colbert: It was confusing for us. We were used to having success and trying to work out why people weren't digging it as much, but by then it was almost too late.

Steve Queralt: We did a tour of America that was really underwhelming, and I think that's when the doubt started to set in, the egos started to rise, and we just got a bit fed up with each other, probably looking for someone to blame.

By the time Ride was in the studio for their fourth album, *Tarantula*, relations between Andy and Mark were so severely strained that Mark walked out on the mixing sessions, and Andy ended up writing and singing all but two of the twelve tracks. With the band announcing their breakup before *Tarantula* even came out, Creation released the widely panned album on March 11, 1996, only to delete it from their catalog a week later. A *Melody Maker* review titled "Eight-Legged Snooze Machine" delighted in their implosion, rhyming "Ride have split, no one gives a flying shit."[3]

Steve Queralt: It was quite a quick breakup. We didn't understand why it wasn't working, but it clearly wasn't. We made a final record to try and save the day, but in my view it's a dreadful album. It was released too quickly, without much enthusiasm, and to top it all off, Creation deleted it on day one.

Loz Colbert: It'd been a very intense period of touring and not much time at home to ground yourself in a form of reality. We'd lost the plot musically, and we needed to have a break from each other. And sure enough we had a very long break.

Their last UK show for twenty years was supporting Oasis in Brighton in December 1994. In an interesting twist, Andy Bell would end up joining Oasis in 1999, playing bass with the Gallagher brothers until their own breakup in 2009.

*

After flirting with Britpop on *Lovelife*, which became their biggest seller as a result, Lush's hopeful career came to a screeching halt in October 1996, when drummer Chris Acland took his own life while visiting his parents in the Lake District in North West England. Even before that tragedy, however, the band was on the verge of imploding.

Emma Anderson: It's not a secret that I wanted to leave the band. There's this obsession to break America that some bands are subjected to by management or labels, and Lush had that from very early on. Touring America is hardcore, and we were just being sent back and back and back. I just got to the point where I thought, *I don't wanna do this anymore*. We were doing this tour with the Gin Blossoms and the Goo Go Dolls, where I just thought, *Why?* Even our fans were saying, "You've already been here twice this year. Why are you back?"

Miki Berenyi: There was quite a storm brewing within the band. Emma was like, "We are not Garbage. We are not No Doubt. We are not the Cranberries. We will never break through in the way this label wants us to." And she was right.

Emma Anderson: I told Phil and Miki I'd had enough. Chris wasn't even there—he was already up in the Lakes with his parents. And then two or three days later Chris died. So that was that. It was a dark, dark time. There's no word for how horrendous it was. I still can't quite get my head around what happened, even all these years later.

Miki Berenyi: I do think that if we had carried on, we probably would've gone way back into the kind of *Split* and *Spooky* stuff, rather than going more commercial. Because I'm an eternal optimist, I'd like to think that we could have actually regrouped, but then Chris died. That's when I thought, *Okay,*

Shoegaze Falls Off a Cliff

well then that's definitely it, 'cause I can't carry on in that band without him.

*

After being dropped from Creation after the release of *Ejector Seat Reservation*, Swervedriver signed a three-album deal with Geffen Records subsidiary DGC Records in 1996, only to be dropped from the label three weeks before their next album, *99th Wonder*, was set for release. Eventually, the album was released in 1998 by Zero Hour Records, which the band toured behind extensively.

Jimmy Hartridge: We exhausted ourselves touring, but the money wasn't there, the momentum wasn't there. In the end we had a meeting on the bus, in Nebraska or somewhere cold, and asked each other, *Is this really worth it? Because it's not really going anywhere.*

Adam Franklin: Basically we were just bored. It was time to do something else. We didn't have any big announcement. It wasn't until about two years later where people started saying, "Is the band still together?"

*

Despite *...XYZ*'s warm critical reception in 1992, Moose's first album didn't sell well, which led to them being dropped from Hut Records two months after release, when parent label Virgin Records was bought out by EMI. After recording a new EP and releasing it on their own label, the band was persuaded to sign with Belgian indie label Play It Again Sam, which released their second album, *Honey Bee*.

Moose McKillop: Play It Again Sam didn't turn out to be the greatest experience. It was very lovely that they picked us up when we'd just been jettisoned, but they weren't the easiest people to communicate with. We did another album, *Live a Little Love a Lot*, and it didn't do well at all. That's when we thought, *Maybe we should have stuck with our own label*.

Moose's success was further stymied by the fact that they had multiple labels for different territories.

Moose McKillop: We basically had three labels that put our material out in different parts of the world, but there was nothing coherent about it. Our second and third albums never had an American release. We'd get communications from people saying, "Why can't I buy your album in this country or that country?" and we never really knew the reason why.

By 1996, after bouncing between labels like a pinball, the defeated Moose recorded a fourth and final album, *High Ball Me!*, which sat on a shelf for years.

Moose McKillop: Things just sort of petered out. A few years go by and you realize that you haven't done anything. There was no split or official end. Finally Russell managed to get the fourth album released in 2000, so it actually saw the light of day.

12 Shoegaze Renaissance

That was supposed to be it. This book should be over. Like "baggy," "C86," "shambling," "romo," "the new wave of new wave," and indeed "The Scene That Celebrates Itself," "shoegaze" was destined to be forgotten as a minor footnote in the largely fabricated music genres created by the underpaid and unserious writers of the British music papers. And as the mid-'90s turned into the new millennium, that's all it was. For the former members of the bands it once described—most of whom had found new careers and lives outside of music—the word "shoegaze" was merely a scar, a faint reminder of their awkward youth.

Simon Scott: You know, for many years it felt like shoegaze was a dirty word. It was this derogatory term people would say with an insulting tone to their voice.

Nathaniel Cramp: I remember trying to talk to Neil about Slowdive and trying to get him to play Slowdive songs around the table, and he wouldn't do it. It was like something you couldn't broach. I think he didn't like to think about it, which is probably indicative of how a lot of people thought about it.

Miki Berenyi: I'm not gonna lie. Not in a million years did I think that anyone would give a shit about Lush twenty years later, not least because of the shit we got at the time.

But then, something started happening. Without warning, a new generation of listeners, mostly young Americans blissfully ignorant of its history, started discovering this music for themselves. And to the bewilderment of Brits who thought the term was deader than disco, everyone was affectionately calling this mysteriously forgotten genre "shoegaze."

Christian Savill: After Slowdive, I moved to America, had kids, and got a normal job. In 2009 or 2010, I was a janitor at Whole Foods in Asheville, North Carolina, and I remember one day I was vacuuming the produce mats when a Slowdive song came on that internal radio that plays around the store. I was like, *This is surreal. I'm vacuuming up bits of lettuce while my past life plays above me.* Word got around that I worked there, so then I'd be collecting carts and some kids would come up and go, "Hey, is it true you used to be in Slowdive?" or "Man, I love *Souvlaki.*"

Adam Franklin: I was living in the States, and I remember being at a shoe shop, funny enough, when my girlfriend says, "Oh, recognize the music?" I couldn't, but it was "99th Dream," the lead track from the fourth Swervedriver album.

Sonic Boom: I toured a fair bit in the US into the noughties, and over the years people would use the "shoegaze" word, and I could tell that they weren't being rude. Somehow it had become a different thing.

Christian Savill: You'd hear new bands coming out and saying, *Hey, we're shoegazers!* In the '90s that would have been like saying, *Hey, we're shit!*

J Mascis: I remember when the Shoegaze guitar pedal came out. Somehow seeing that pedal seemed to give it a more positive light.

So when and how did this shoegaze sea change happen? Lacking any singular big bang event to explain the genre's revival, people have pointed to a handful of factors, the most obvious being the advent of the internet.

Moose McKillop: I'm not surprised that people like it, because it's great music. I'm just surprised it actually found a way to another generation, but then I suppose the internet is the answer to that.

Greg Ackell: It used to be that a band at our level would make a record, and once the records are out of print and you stop touring, it would just disappear forever. It'd be some deep archival dive to find it again. The way that everything is discoverable now, there's an audience there.

Neil Halstead: It allows these kids to discover shoegaze music on their own. You go down a rabbit hole and end up on the Pale Saints or whatever. Without the internet, it would never have happened.

Sonic Boom: I mean, no one would remember Spacemen 3 for two seconds if it wasn't for the internet. We weren't a super big band when we split up, but I guess some things find their natural habitat further afield. Sometimes it's America, sometimes it's Japan . . .

The world of cinema also helped keep shoegaze alive through the dark years. American indie films like Hal Hartley's *Amateur* (1994) and Quinton Peeples' *Joyride* (1996) both heavily feature shoegaze music in their soundtracks. Director Gregg Araki has consistently relied on shoegaze throughout his filmography, with 1992's *The Living End* and 1997's *Nowhere* even taking their names from releases by the Jesus and Mary Chain and Ride, and 2004's *Mysterious Skin* featuring original scoring by Robin Guthrie. Inspired by Wong Kar Wai's 1994 movie *Chungking Express*—which itself uses a shoegazey visual style and features Cocteau Twins and Cranberries songs sung in Cantonese—director Sofia Coppola recruited Kevin Shields to soundtrack and score her Oscar-winning 2003 film, *Lost in Translation*, which has since been credited for helping reawaken the shoegaze sound in America and even bringing about the eventual reformations of My Bloody Valentine and the Jesus and Mary Chain.

In 2002, German record label Morr Music released a two-disc tribute album titled *Blue Skied an' Clear*, featuring indie electronic artists covering Slowdive songs—many of whom were specifically inspired by their leftfield flop, *Pygmalion*. The following year, one of those artists, ambient techno producer Ulrich Schnauss, released the album *A Strangely Isolated Place*, which hears him openly adapting the influence of My Bloody Valentine, Cocteau Twins, and their shoegaze spawn into an IDM world. Schnauss is "not the least bit concerned about hiding his influences," Chris Ott wrote in a since deleted review for *Pitchfork*, but "he is most obviously obsessed with Slowdive . . . I can only assume Morr's *Blue Skied An' Clear* tribute to those shoegazers was his idea."[1]

A month prior, French electronic duo M83 released their hugely acclaimed second album, *Dead Cities, Red Seas & Lost Ghosts*, which elicited widespread comparisons to My Bloody Valentine. Drawing upon the same vocabulary critics used to describe the original shoegaze releases, *Pitchfork's* Matt LeMay wrote of *Dead Cities*: "The sound is absolutely huge, its relentless attention to detail eclipsed only by the stunning emotional power it conveys. For fifty-seven glorious minutes, its impossibly intricate tapestry of buzzing techno synthesizers, distorted electric guitars, cheesy drum machines, and subdued vocals generate a sense of bodily movement through a landscape of beauty, disappointment, glory, and decrepitude."[2]

Nathaniel Cramp: The sound was out there. There was lots of ambient and electronic stuff. There were little echoes in all the post-rock stuff, like Mogwai and Sigur Rós. That isn't a million miles away from Slowdive, is it?

That same year, *Pitchfork* published its updated "Top 100 Albums of the 1990s," which placed My Bloody Valentine's *Loveless* at number 2, behind Radiohead's *OK Computer*. Making clear to young indie rock fans (this author included) that this music contains some sacred alchemy beyond human comprehension, Mark Richardson lamented, "I've long dreamt of an album that was 'Like *Loveless*, but more,' but I haven't found it."[3]

Alan McGee: I think it was *Pitchfork* that decided these bands are great and then they got a whole generation of kids back into it.

Throughout the 2000s, shoegaze became an increasingly referenced genre for listeners and new musicians alike, with the label loosely applied to releases like Jesu's *Jesu* (2004), Autolux's *Future Perfect* (2004), Asobi Seksu's *Citrus* (2006), Blonde Redhead's *23* (2007), the self-titled debuts of A Place to Bury Strangers (2007) and the Pains of Being Pure at Heart (2009), and A Sunny Day in Glasgow's *Ashes Grammar* (2009).

By the 2010s, the word "shoegaze"—as well as the cringeworthy "nu-gaze"—was being applied to an increasingly broad spectrum of artists, ranging from more obvious descendants like DIIV, Deerhunter, Beach House, Nothing, No Joy, Ringo Deathstarr, and Spirit of the Beehive, to more far-flung ones like Deafheaven, whose black metal and shoegaze fusing 2013 album, *Sunbather*, popularized the term "blackgaze." You can also find shoegaze bands from all around the world, such as Resplandor (Peru), Gnoomes (Russia), Tokyo Shoegazer (Japan), Flyying Colours (Australia), Echo Ladies (Sweden), and Lucid Express (Hong Kong).

Today you even have shoegaze specific record labels like Sonic Cathedral—"The label that celebrates itself"—run by former *NME* sub-editor Nathaniel Cramp, which was born out of a series of club nights he began organizing in 2004. The events, which would include DJ sets from veterans like Lush's Emma Anderson and live performances from contemporary acts like the Radio Dept, were an instant hit.

Shoegaze

Nathaniel Cramp: I had no idea that so many people would come. Some of them were wearing original Chapterhouse T-shirts. It was like they'd been locked indoors for ten years and finally got let out to play.

Morphing into a label after 2006, Sonic Cathedral has released exciting new shoegaze from bands like bdrmm, Whitelands, and deary, not to mention solo albums from Emma Anderson, Slowdive's Neil Halstead, and Ride's Andy Bell.

But the fact that the shoegaze sound came back doesn't necessarily explain why new artists began using the word "shoegaze"—which the original groups plainly rejected—to describe themselves. That very well might have something to do with a now obsolete social media platform that launched in 2003.

Adam Franklin: You remember how on MySpace you could have your own personal page, but then you'd also have your band page? You could say, *Yeah, we're a band from blah, blah, blah*, and then there was a genre selection with a dropdown tab that had *blues, jazz, metal, funk, disco* . . . and then *shoegaze*. I thought, *That's hilarious*, because before then shoegaze must have been the most unpopular thing of all time.

Rachel Goswell: It was on MySpace where I became aware that shoegaze had become an actual genre that bands were using to describe their sound. I was a bit taken aback, thinking, *Oh my God, this is so weird.*

Backing up this shoegaze rebirth, a Google Ngram search charting the appearance of "shoegaze" in print between 1990 and 2019 shows a sharp uptick after 2002.

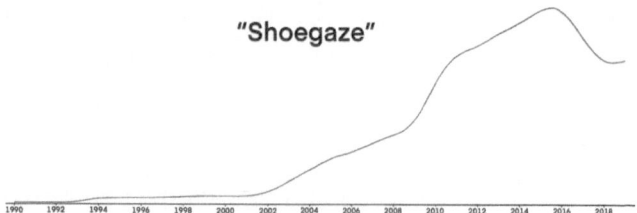

"Shoegaze"

1990 1992 1994 1996 1998 2000 2002 2004 2006 2008 2010 2012 2014 2016 2018

For the still traumatized survivors of shoegaze's first wave, the change in meaning took some adjusting to.

Simon Scott: It was like, *Wow, maybe it isn't such a dirty word after all.*

Andy Sherriff: I think all of those first bands still probably wince a little bit at being called shoegaze, but we're all aware that it's a positive association now.

Neil Halstead: I love it now, and I love the fact that it's been reclaimed.

Steve Queralt: Now it's a real badge of honor to be called a shoegaze band. To be reminded that you were there from the start, and that you maybe made one of the best, most recognizable shoegaze albums ever, I'm immensely proud of that.

Once they accepted it, the original shoegazers finally found an audience who appreciated their previously ostracized music without any of the baggage it once carried.

Miki Berenyi: Thank god for America, because otherwise it would never have become a term of affection. It was really that misunderstanding that made it so.

Chris Roberts: In America, where you have a different cultural context, you have a younger generation, who perhaps weren't even born when the *Melody Maker* and *NME* were doing these reviews. They're hearing it with open ears, with a fresh perspective, and taking it on the music's own sake, rather than through the personalities and attitudes of the time.

Nathaniel Cramp: Once enough time had passed, people could appreciate the music for what it was, with no context or negativity.

More recently, TikTok has done for Gen Z what MySpace did for millennials in the early 2000s, with publications like *Vice* observing how legions of teens are once again resurrecting the genre to soundtrack their "bleak, post-COVID world,"[4] and *Stereogum* crediting the platform for making shoegaze "bigger than ever."[5] As of late 2023—around the time a *Pitchfork* think piece declared it the year "The Shoegaze Revival Hit Its Stride"[6]—the TikTok hashtag #shoegaze has tallied up nearly 700 million views, while #slowdive and #mybloodyvalentine have racked up 200 and 140 million views respectively.

Robin Guthrie: I sometimes get to see the demographics of who's buying my music, and it's an awful lot of people under thirty-five. Considering some of these records were made forty years ago, these people are literally discovering something from another era, which is a difficult thing for me to get my head around, but it's great because if I had any master plan, it was to make records that were timeless.

Miki Berenyi: I have to remind myself that kids getting into shoegaze today is like me getting into '60s garage bands and the *Nuggets* collections when I was growing up.

David Quantick: I can't imagine Britpop coming back, but with shoegaze there's something to discover. It doesn't give away all its secrets straight away. It's mysterious, and that appeals to a certain kind of person.

Greg Ackell: Young people are the finders of lost causes. They want to find something that's theirs, that belongs to them. So why not pick up the lost cause, the thing that didn't get its due, as the thing that's gonna define you as a music fan?

*

Of course, the most feel-good part of the shoegaze renaissance is how many of the original bands got back together as a result. As was only appropriate, My Bloody Valentine started the trend when, in 2007, they announced their first live shows in sixteen years.

Nathaniel Cramp: MBV getting back together was a big deal. They were always kind of above criticism, but it obviously allowed people to think about their influence and other bands that were around at the same time or just afterwards.

Six years later—the blink of an eye in Valentine time—with absolutely zero warning, they finally dropped their third album, *m b v*, a full twenty-two years after *Loveless*, which received the universal acclaim they were used to.

Adam Franklin: I remember the night MBV finally released a follow-up to *Loveless*, and it kind of just snuck out online. I thought it was great that they did it that way, rather than doing it with some big sort of rollout the way that any other band of the music industry would do. In some ways it's more epic because they did it that way.

As of this book's writing, the band continues to tour and tease new music, which may or may not arrive this decade.

*

After Chapterhouse's Andy, Stephen, and Ashley Bates found steady careers as film composers and sound designers—while Simon Rowe played in Neil and Rachel's post-Slowdive band Mojave 3—the group briefly reformed between 2008 and 2010.

Andy Sherriff: We got asked by Ulrich Schnauss to play at a festival he was doing after he'd done a cover of "Love Forever." We'd always talked about doing a tour of Japan and America, where we were still popular, so we thought, *Why not?*

Although the experience was largely positive, they happily returned to their more lucrative and consistent day jobs afterward and remain close friends.

*

After a ten-year hiatus, during which Adam remained active with various solo projects and Jimmy founded a music distribution company, Swervedriver started playing shows again in 2008, beginning with a comeback gig at that year's Coachella.

Adam Franklin: It wasn't a spectacular gig, but the more exciting thing was getting back in the rehearsal room and saying, "Right, well what song should we do then?" And somebody calls out a song. "Alright, let's see if we can remember it." And then you're surprised that it comes back.

Jimmy Hartridge: We did a tour of America, and it was clear that a new generation quite appreciated it. It was a really good tour, so we kept on doing it.

After more touring, not to mention a somewhat random performance on *Late Night with Jimmy Fallon*, the band finally got around to recording new music, resulting in 2015's *I Wasn't Born to Lose You* and 2019's *Future Ruins*.

Adam Franklin: *I Wasn't Born To Lose You* is my favorite Swervedriver album. The last song on it, "I Wonder," is Swervedriver being more shoegaze than we ever were in the '90s.

*

After years of fielding offers to reform while focusing on various other projects, the boys in Ride got back together in 2015 with a brief run of big festival dates that included stops at Coachella and Primavera Sound, with no intention to keep going.

Steve Queralt: That first time where we headlined the main stage at Primavera was a huge triumph for me personally.

Loz Colbert: The amount of people and the fact that we could just see we were connecting with a bigger crowd than we'd ever had the first time around—it was a glorious moment. That made us hungry to come back again and try and make something new, because we felt like the magic hadn't really gone.

Since then they've recorded three new albums—with *Clash's* Robin Murray calling their latest, 2024's *Interplay*, "perhaps the best album yet of their mighty second arc"—while playing their classic shoegaze albums in full for new generations of fans.

Mark Gardener: It's been really interesting playing those records again, as men now. I'm not as pretty as I used to be, but I'm a much better musician and singer now, and we're a much stronger band. We're still going because there's still a real call for it.

*

After years of resisting the call, the surviving members of Lush reunited in 2016 for a huge tour across Europe and America, though it may not have been the best idea.

Miki Berenyi: I'm not gonna lie, it ended as a fucking disaster, mainly because there was a massive fight. Emma and Phil still don't talk to me.

Emma Anderson: It was horrible, and it probably should never have happened. I thought we were gonna do an album, two albums, three albums, but it didn't turn out like that.

Despite the fallout, the reunion had its silver linings.

Emma Anderson: We played two sold-out nights at the Roundhouse in London, which was amazing. There were young people and teenagers there who hadn't even been born when we put out our first record.

Miki Berenyi: I am massively grateful for that reunion. After Chris died I spent twenty years not doing music, because I just couldn't deal with it. However fucking hard that tour was, it got me back into playing music. I was genuinely surprised at how happy it made me.

Emma Anderson: We put out the [*Blind Spot*] EP, and 4AD put out the *Chorus* and *Origami* box sets, and we got some really good reviews for them. It was really refreshing seeing people just talk about the music.

Afterward, Miki formed Piroshka with Moose from Moose— with whom she has two kids—along with Elastica drummer Justin Welch and Modern English bassist Mick Conroy. (In 2024, Miki, Moose, and Conroy also began touring, sans Welch, as the Miki Berenyi Trio.) Meanwhile, Emma released her debut solo album, *Pearlies*, in the fall of 2023, shortly after being interviewed for this book.

Miki Berenyi: Doing the Lush reunion for the music, and now being in a new band for the music—because you certainly don't make any fucking money at it—is like going back to when I was first in a band, where I never expected to make it, I never expected to go to America, I never expected to sign to 4AD. I got into it because it seemed fun and I enjoyed it, and now it feels like it's all the way back to that, which is the way it should be.

*

While Russell and Moose (the man) are still dear friends, Russell now lives a private life in Portugal and has no interest in reviving Moose (the band). As of writing, UK indie label Bella

Union is working to release a box set finally gathering their scattered discography in one place.

*

After leaving music completely behind after Drop Nineteens' underwhelming second album, *National Coma*, Greg Ackell spent twenty-five years selling flowers in New York City.

Greg Ackell: I'd see someone at a show or someone would call me, and they would try to tempt me to do something with Drop Nineteens again. I would just say, "You're outta your fucking mind." I was so done with that part of my life.

Then, one day, something changed.

Greg Ackell: This one time I got off the phone, and I just started thinking, *What would a modern Drop Nineteens single sound like?* I hadn't asked myself that question before. So I texted Steve, who's still my best friend and partner in this, and I think he'd been kind of waiting for years for me to say that. As we approached the other band members, I got a similar feeling. They all felt the time was right.

After generating a tidal wave of press in early 2022 with the mere announcement that they were reforming, Drop Nineteens released their third album, *Hard Light*, in November 2023 to positive reviews, with *Under the Radar* calling it "an immensely satisfying return that evokes the slacker tone and overdriven sound of their debut while illuminating the lyrical heart of a band changed by time, often for the better."[7]

*

No comeback has been more triumphant than that of Slowdive, who broke up as one of shoegaze's most pitiful pariahs, only to return as the biggest headliner of the bunch.

Rachel Goswell: We'd been asked about reforming once or twice before, and for years I was like, *I don't ever wanna reform Slowdive. It's pointless.*

Neil Halstead: We got contacted by Primavera, and I don't think we took it very seriously initially.

Christian Savill: I'd seen Chapterhouse reform and I thought, *That looks fun.* But I never thought Neil would want to get it back together, so I was really shocked when he got in touch.

Simon Scott: The phone rang in 2013, and Christian said, "Hey, there's people offering us gigs. I don't know if you're free, but we were thinking of doing it."

Christian Savill: I remember when we got on the Primavera lineup poster and we saw the billing. I was like, *Holy shit, is this for real?*

Rachel Goswell: I don't think any of us understood how big Slowdive had become in our absence until we were about to walk on stage in Barcelona. I remember we were waiting to go on when the backdrop with our name on it came down. The audience just erupted and we stood there going, *That's a lot of people . . .* I was literally shaking throughout the entire gig, loving it, and thinking, *Fuck yeah*, but equally terrified.

Nick Chaplin: There's a story we've told a hundred times where, in the '90s, we knew the game was up when we were playing a gig and, before we even finished, there was a woman with a bucket, mopping up the floor around about the ten people that were still there. So to go from that to playing in front of tens of thousands of people . . .

Neil Halstead: We ended up doing a whole bunch of festivals that year. Doing the shows was really brilliant. And from the first rehearsal when we got back together, and having Simon back, it was kind of like, *Oh yeah, this is really good. This is great.* That carried into the idea of doing a record.

Rachel Goswell: We went in to do that record with no expectations. We didn't have a record label. We didn't want any outside pressure. It was just like, *Let's just go and see what we can do and whether we enjoy the process*, which we did.

Nathaniel Cramp: The new record that they made in 2017 was their best. I think it's one of the best shoegaze records there's been. Then they followed it with [2023's] *everything is alive*, which elevated them higher than ever, all the way to number 3 in the Billboard charts, which would have been unthinkable a few years ago.

Nick Chaplin: We're constantly surprised by how well the music and the band is received now. We've gone to countries that we never went to in the '90s: Japan, Australia, Southeast Asia, South America.

Paul Lester: Slowdive reforming ready did surprise me. It would be like Jerry and the Pacemakers suddenly becoming a hit in 1990 and playing on the same bill as the Stone Roses and Ride.

Steve Sutherland: They've been reappraised, and they're more appreciated now than they were at the time. My daughter, who's twenty-one, is way more into Slowdive than I ever was.

Polly Birkbeck: Slowdive is more popular than ever. My daughter, who's seventeen, has them on her Spotify.

Alan McGee: To tell you the truth, I don't think I really got Slowdive. I got it on a level, but I think they were a lot better than I ever thought they were, and they went on to prove that, 'cause they're the biggest one now. They're bigger than the Valentines. I'm really happy for them that, through the internet, people found their music and they found their audience twenty-fucking-five years later.

Nathaniel Cramp: Revenge is too strong a word, but it felt like vindication to turn what ended very negatively for them into something so positive. It reframed their whole story.

Adam Franklin: There's certainly a sense of vindication with how successful all these bands have been since they got back together.

Mark Gardener: It was vindicating when the ones that came back showed they could do it again, because they were *always* good. As far as the English press are concerned, a lot of those papers are dead now, so we have the last laugh. It's thirty years on, and we're still playing those records, still filling rooms, and getting new audiences coming through.

Christian Savill: We didn't expect to have this come around again. We already learned that these things can be fleeting, so we're just enjoying it, making the most of it, and taking everything as it happens, because I could be back working the tills anytime.

13 The Legacy of Shoegaze

So what is it about this badly defined, short-lived, once-hated, certainly-not-for-everyone music that continues to earn new fans and inspire new artists in its image?

Chris Roberts: It's not overtly political. It's not trying to convey a message about the world. It's maybe a little narcissistic and navel-gazing—not to mention shoegazing—but there's a beauty in there. It speaks to other people, sometimes because it touches emotions that previous, safer sounds had not touched, and in that way, it added to the vocabulary of music.

Nathaniel Cramp: The '80s and the end of the Thatcher era had been a pretty unsettling decade. The fact that shoegaze appeared around a similar time as rave music, when people were looking for escapism, is maybe not a coincidence. Maybe that's why it's come back. People just want to get lost and escape from all the bad stuff that is happening.

Mark Gardener: It's all about escape, sometimes from rough, dark times. It can help you get lost in the space that those atmospheric, widescreen sounds create.

Simon Scott: The music's full of moments of being insecure and frightened and overwhelmed, and I think there's a beauty in being carried away by this tidal wave of sound and emotion. Particularly in America, people seem quite perceptive of the fact that there's insecurity in shoegaze. It's fine to feel vulnerable and just be carried away by this huge wall of sound, these moments of fragility and devastating noise.

Rachel Goswell: For me it's my happy place, where I feel most normal. It feels like home.

Alan Moulder: Maybe it's come back because there's so much pop that's very straightforward and direct, and it's nice to have something that's a bit more obtuse. It's something you can immerse yourself in, rather than just having one dimension.

Andy Sherriff: Sometimes you have to work a little bit to discover the best music. If it's right in your face, then you get bored of it quickly. If you have to work a little bit to get into something, it gives you greater and longer lasting pleasure.

Steve Sutherland: It's made by kids with guitars and drums, but apart from that, it's got very little affiliation to the rules of pop. It doesn't have any of the ciphers or symbols that traditional pop has—the lyric, the riffs, the posturing, the personality—so, in a weird way, it's of no time and it's timeless.

Neil Halstead: We were all trying to take guitar music and do something new and different with every record we were making. That was how we approached it every time we went into the studio, because that was what our heroes did with their music.

Jimmy Hartridge: I think shoegaze was one of the last, if not *the* last, guitar-led art forms that was trying to do something that was brand new. Even though it borrowed heavily from the Velvet Underground and stuff, I think the shoegaze bands were trying to push the boundaries. I mean, there's nothing like *Loveless*. It was a new format, and I can't think of anything rock-wise that has been new since then.

Adam Franklin: The thing that we loved about the *Pebbles* and *Nuggets* records was that these were one-off songs recorded by bands that never got anywhere. Nobody knew who they were—they were failed bands—but this music was fantastic and fed something new twenty years later.

Greg Ackell: You know that F. Scott Fitzgerald line about how a sentimental person sees a good thing and wishes it will last forever, but a romantic person sees a good thing and has the desperate confidence that it won't? The idea being that something has to be lost for it to have value. Maybe the fact that shoegaze was lost—the way it was unceremoniously cut off and didn't get its due—gives it some value. Maybe that's one of the reasons it's coming back.

At the risk of overly romanticizing shoegaze, there also seems to be a certain purity to the music and the bands that make it.

Sonic Boom: People ask me now, *What would you do if you wanted to be a successful band?* I think the thing to do is be uncompromising and don't change your music if you think it's any good. It doesn't matter what anyone else says to you. You need to have that strength and conviction, even if it might not resonate with people that week, that year, or even that decade. I think that's one of the secrets of why people still care about Spacemen 3. It was done with a certain purity, where we decided this was our path and we stuck to it.

Paul Lester: In most music scenes, the ambition is to be as big as the Beatles, whereas I don't know if they had that with shoegaze. I think these people just wanted to make nice sounds on the guitar and see where it took them. It was an interesting model for how to sustain an alternative music scene for a time.

Steve Sutherland: We as journalists completely got it wrong, because we always assumed that the best thing in the world would be for the bands we discovered to become really, really big. In my era as an *NME* editor we had a great time, sold loads of magazines, and helped sell loads of records, but it was a bad idea, because the bands became really, really big and really, really bad. At one point Oasis wanted to be the best band in the world, and then suddenly they wanted to be the biggest band in the world, and that's not the same thing. At one time My Bloody Valentine was the best band in the world, but they never wanted to be the biggest band in the world, and then they went away.

Andy Sherriff: I think we had *different* ambitions, rather than being *less* ambitious. I was never interested in fame. Obviously you want people to hear your music, but sometimes people just wanna be famous and they don't care how.

Robin Guthrie: We didn't like the idea of celebrity. That would've been embarrassing. I can't speak for other people, but I don't think Liz and I really wanted that. We were just hiding behind this allure of what we did with our sound, and it left people guessing about who we were while we had our little private world.

Miki Berenyi: It was possibly a more innocent time, certainly a less cynical time. I don't think most of those bands ever expected to be playing Wembley Stadium. They were a bit purer about what they were doing. I don't think it was such a plotted career path like it became later.

Mark Gardener: People are trying too hard to make a career, and as soon as you think about that, it kills it in a way. Of course we wanted to do alright, but it wasn't calculated in that way. For me, it was pure expression.

Neil Halstead: I mean, we never had a chance to sell out. It wasn't like, *If you do this, it'll get played on the radio.* No one's ever gonna play this on the radio, so you may as well make it sound as shitty or as weird as you want. It was always just about trying to make an interesting record.

Ian Masters: None of us were particularly good musicians, but we just had endless enthusiasm and aspirations to make good music. The way we presented ourselves on stage was because we were having to concentrate in order not to fuck things up. The band itself was almost entirely unimportant. Only the music that we were making—if it succeeded in making something larger than the sum of its parts—was important.

Jimmy Hartridge: That's the point of the term shoegaze, isn't it? That these guys are more interested in fiddling around with their amps, or turning the bass and fuzz up, than they are with engaging with their audience and being a proper rockstar? There's no "Thank you very much" or "Let's rock!" It's just noise and melody, which is enough for me, but doesn't really translate to the masses. It's really just art for art's sake.

Emma Anderson: Even more so than a lot of the Madchester or grunge bands, shoegaze has actually stood the test of time, and I think that says quite a lot. It's funny because back in the late '80s and early '90s, we very much felt that we were in the shadow of the Mary Chain, My Bloody Valentine, and the Cocteau Twins, whereas now it feels that we are the precursors and there's other bands in our shadow. So two fingers up to all the doubters.

And while it's impossible to measure the true scale of its influence, you can hear shoegaze's legacy everywhere if you listen for it.

Steve Queralt: Shoegaze never really died. It never really shone as bright as Britpop or grunge, which shined so brightly but didn't last long. Shoegaze just faded away in a long burst of reverb, and then came back.

Paul Lester: It was like this explosion, and then all these scintilla and tiny little crystal shards with slight differences between them went flying everywhere. Some of the shards ended up in America, some ended up in Europe, some ended up in Japan.

Andy Bell: It's not a sound that's tied to a particular place. I've heard amazing takes on the shoegaze tropes from Japan and South America. Almost everywhere in the world that you can think of, there have been bands trying it out.

Steve Queralt: Shoegaze has gone beyond guitars. It's gone beyond rock music. It's become a term that can cover all sorts of music, from new classical artists like Jóhann Jóhannsson to electronica bands like Boards of Canada. It's so inclusive it's difficult to describe.

Stephen Patman: At the time it was a word created to describe maybe five bands. Now it's become a big umbrella that encompasses bands that have a larger-than-life aesthetic or an otherworldliness to their sound. There are little elements of shoegaze mixed in with quite normal mainstream records. Even Lizzo has a track, "Juice," that has a shoegazey guitar. I'm always very surprised about what is considered to be shoegaze these days. It's become something that doesn't belong to me anymore.

Polly Birkbeck: The legacy is the fact that it's a recognized genre now. It has a Wikipedia page. Young kids can aspire to be a shoegazing band without being mocked. It will probably always be there, alongside new wave, Britpop, and grunge.

Simon Scott: It's strange and makes us blush, but people say things like, "You guys are legends!" It feels really weird for us to be perceived that way, but what's really fantastic is when we play shows and you see groups of people in their twenties, even in their teens, and they're forming bands because they love Slowdive and they're inspired to go out and buy a guitar. It's lovely to have that full circle where we've influenced people in the same way we were influenced.

So what's your definition of shoegaze?

Alan McGee: I don't think I know what shoegaze is. Spacey, melodic rock and roll?

David Quantick: Introspective, moody guitar music with lots of effects pedals that sounds like the Cocteau Twins on a depressed day.

J Mascis: Bands inspired by My Bloody Valentine and trying to add their own twist to it.

Moose McKillop: You have to say: Distortion? *Check.* Reverb? *Check.* Delay? *Check.* Quieter vocals? *Check.* Two guitarists? *Three would be better.*

Jimmy Hartridge: It should have been called something like "avant-garde heavy indie rock."

Neil Halstead: I would've called it "progressive psychedelic guitar music," but that doesn't sound cool.

Polly Birkbeck: Swirly, fuzzy guitars with ethereal, dreamy effects.

Greg Ackell: Dense, romantic, understated guitar music.

Nick Chaplin: Atmospheric, experimental guitar music.

Simon Scott: Hazy, thickly textured, blurred sonic immersiveness.

Sonic Boom: An awesome, shiny, droney, environment of sound.

Mark Gardener: The juxtaposition of beautiful melodies and harmonies against noise and atmosphere.

Christian Savill: Melancholic pop music with big washes of sound and otherworldly guitar made by people who are a bit shy.

Nathaniel Cramp: A beautiful, textured, enveloping sound that you can lose yourself in.

Rachel Goswell: Walls of sound.

Paul Lester: Reveling in sound for its own sake.

Robin Guthrie: Beautiful noise.

Alan Moulder: Beauty and violence.

Andy Sherriff: A particular concoction of noise and melody.

Loz Colbert: Noise. It always seems to come back to that.

Andy Bell: It's more of a production style or an overall feel than a specific sound.

Steve Queralt: It's outgrown its definition. It's just a feeling.

Steve Sutherland: The priority of music over lyrical content, atmosphere over didactics, sound over message, with the goal of becoming lost in it and hearing things that only you hear.

Jane Savidge: A scene that didn't care about anything or anybody.

Chris Roberts: A sometimes indulgent genre that explored brave areas and stretched sonic boundaries; a necessary reaction to the blander music of the time that has, against all odds, found that its echoes and ghosts live on thirty years later.

Ian Masters: I really couldn't give a fuck about the word "shoegaze." It was lazy journalism then, and it's lazy journalism now. It seems like a dearth of vocabulary to describe music with one word, so that's not something I'm interested in.

Emma Anderson: The word "shoegazing" seemed so ridiculous at the time, but it stuck, and now I don't mind it at all. In fact, I've grown very fond of it.

Adam Franklin: The thing about shoegaze bands, of course, is that they're always reluctant to say anything. So I suppose the truest definition would just be to shrug.

Afterword

While writing this manuscript, I found myself reflecting on something Steve Sutherland said to me while discussing the notion of a book on shoegaze.

"There are two different ways of looking at it," he said. "There's the Henry Rollins way, where you say there should be no such thing as rare music. He's spent his whole life trying to bring bands like Suicide to the public, and he loathes the idea of the record collector rarity."

"Then there's the other side," Sutherland continued, "the Morrissey thing, where we hate it when our friends become successful. Shoegaze is a secret society, and it was always best appreciated as a secret society. As soon as too many people started to infringe upon it, it ruined it, and indie kids hate it when other people discover their music, because it's not theirs anymore."

He concluded, "Shoegaze wasn't designed for millions of people to appreciate, and yet you are writing a book that might turn a lot of people onto it when it might be best left hiding under a rock. You could be the villain in this piece."

I first pitched this book not because I knew a lot about shoegaze or was even passionate about it but because I *didn't* know much about it, no one else seemed to either, and that intrigued me. Like the music itself, there was something hidden and mysterious about the shoegaze story, and that drew me in.

If shoegaze music has one constant for me, it is its beauty. The melodies are beautiful, the noise is beautiful, and, to my surprise, the history is even beautiful in its humility, its purity of intentions, and its redemptive comeback.

Reflecting upon Steve's words—which may hold more or less weight considering that he, the editor who gave us "The Scene That Celebrates Itself" and "The Battle of Britpop," could also be painted as a villain in the shoegaze story—I recognize that by exposing shoegaze to air, I risk tarnishing its mysterious powers.

As a sentimental type who has at times fallen prey to the Morrissey train of thought, I hear the little voice that says this music would be best hidden away for a small club who can call it their own. But as we all know by now, Morrissey is a misguided twat, in spite of his own beautiful music.

I prefer to believe in the school of Rollins: that beautiful music like this ought to be shared, and it's been plain to see that any original shoegazer relishes the fact that new generations have come to appreciate the art they made three decades ago.

By its very nature, which both attracts and repels, shoegaze is at no risk of becoming too popular, nor is it in any danger of ever disappearing again. Shoegaze is too busy staring down at its feet, and it doesn't give a fuck whether you're paying attention or not.

Ryan Pinkard, Summer 2023

10 Essential Tracks

For those who skipped straight here before reading the book, shoegaze is not a particularly song-focused genre but rather one best understood through albums and EPs. Thus, in addition to the "10 Essential Tracks" included in all Genre series titles, this book features lists of essential albums and EPs from shoegaze's first wave, as well as a list of "modern shoegaze" LPs curated by Sonic Cathedral's Nathaniel Cramp. May these highly subjective but lovingly chosen recordings act as a springboard for your own journey into the shoegaze ether. **—RP**

10 Essential Tracks
"You Made Me Realise" by My Bloody Valentine
"Soon" by My Bloody Valentine
"Sight of You" by Pale Saints
"Sweetness and Light" by Lush
"Pearl" by Chapterhouse
"Vapour Trail" by Ride
"When the Sun Hits" by Slowdive
"Jack" by Moose
"Duel" by Swervedriver
"Winona" by Drop Nineteens

Further Listening

"Leave Them All Behind" by Ride

"Dreams Burn Down" by Ride

"Catch the Breeze" by Slowdive

"Autosleeper" by Chapterhouse

"Nothing Natural" by Lush

"Suzanne" by Moose

"Kick the Tragedy" by Drop Nineteens

"Never Lose That Feeling" by Swervedriver

"Kinky Love" by Pale Saints

"Black Metallic" by Catherine Wheel

"Skyscraper" by The Boo Radleys

"Star Sail" by The Verve

"Sing" by Blur

"Everso" by The Telescopes

"Liar" by The Charlottes

"There's No Such Thing as Black Orchids" by Lilys

"Jeremy Parker" by Swirlies

"Sunshine Smile" by Adorable

"Drive That Fast" by Kitchens of Distinction

"Sleep" by Eternal

10 Essential EPs

You Made Me Realise by My Bloody Valentine

Tremolo by My Bloody Valentine

Mad Love by Lush

Holding Our Breath by Slowdive

Jack by Moose

Flesh Balloon by Pale Saints

Today Forever by Ride

Sunburst by Chapterhouse

Son of Mustang Ford by Swervedriver

Your Aquarium by Drop Nineteens

Further Listening

Glider by My Bloody Valentine

Ride by Ride

Play by Ride

Fall by Ride

Slowdive by Slowdive

Morningrise by Slowdive

Outside Your Room by Slowdive

5EP by Slowdive

Freefall by Chapterhouse

Cool Breeze by Moose

Barging into the Presence of God by Pale Saints

Rave Down by Swervedriver

45 by Revolver

Painful Thing by Catherine Wheel

Drive That Fast by Kitchens of Distinction

Snag by Bleach

Aruca by Medicine

Frozen by Curve

Blindfold by Curve

Cherry by Curve

10 Essential Albums

Isn't Anything by My Bloody Valentine

Loveless by My Bloody Valentine

Nowhere by Ride

Going Blank Again by Ride

Souvlaki by Slowdive

Mezcal Head by Swervedriver

Whirlpool by Chapterhouse

Spooky by Lush

The Comforts of Madness by Pale Saints

Delaware by Drop Nineteens

Further Listening

Just for a Day by Slowdive
Pygmalion by Slowdive
Raise by Swervedriver
...XYZ by Moose
Strange Free World by Kitchens of Distinction
Ferment by Catherine Wheel
Everything's Alright Forever by The Boo Radleys
Blonder Tongue Audio Baton by Swirlies
Shot Forth Self Living by Medicine
Lido by Th' Faith Healers
A Storm in Heaven by The Verve
Quique by Seefeel
Against Perfection by Adorable
Gold by Starflyer 59
Doppelgänger by Curve
In the Presence of Nothing by Lilys
Taste by The Telescopes
69 by A. R. Kane
Wings of Joy by Cranes
Stereo Musicale by Blind Mr. Jones

Modern Shoegaze Favorites

A Strangely Isolated Place by Ulrich Schnauss
Three Fact Fader by Engineers
Lesser Matters by The Radio Dept.
m b v by My Bloody Valentine
Slowdive by Slowdive
Weather Diaries by Ride
Dead Cities, Red Seas & Lost Ghosts by M83
Hard Light by Drop Nineteens
Serena-Maneesh 2: Abyss in B Minor by Serena-Maneesh
Wait to Pleasure by No Joy

Further Listening

A Place to Bury Strangers by A Place to Bury Strangers

Disconnect from Desire by School of Seven Bells

Citrus by Asobi Seksu

23 by Blonde Redhead

Future Perfect by Autolux

Ashes Grammar by A Sunny Day in Glasgow

Pink Noise by Echo Ladies

Jesu by Jesu

Balance by Lorelle Meets the Obsolete

Bedroom by bdrmm

This Is Not a Safe Place by Ride

I Wasn't Born to Lose You by Swervedriver

Halcyon Digest by Deerhunter

Oshin by DIIV

Souvenirs D'un Autre Monde by Alcest

Bright to Death by Film School

Colour Trip by Ringo Deathstarr

Picturesque by MOLLY

Tired of Tomorrow by Nothing

Everything Is Alive by Slowdive

Acknowledgments

This book is indebted to the individuals who generously granted me the time to stroll down memory lane. My biggest thanks to Greg Ackell, Emma Anderson, Andy Bell, Miki Berenyi, Polly Birkbeck, Loz Colbert, Nick Chaplin, Nathaniel Cramp, Adam Franklin, Mark Gardener, Rachel Goswell, Robin Guthrie, Neil Halstead, Jimmy Hartridge, Sonic Boom, Paul Lester, J Mascis, Alan McGee, Moose McKillop, Alan Moulder, Stephen Patman, David Quantick, Steve Queralt, Chris Roberts, Jane Savidge, Christian Savill, Simon Scott, Andy Sherriff, and Steve Sutherland.

Additional thanks to Miki, Rachel, Russell Beresford, Florence Guthrie, Al Mills, and Rich Walker for helping make many of these conversations happen; to My Bloody Valentine for ignoring my emails; to Tana for always being my first and last reader; to the great Stephen Deusner for his generous and thoughtful notes; and to my editor, Nat Cramp for his invaluable expertise and for doing more than anyone to keep shoegaze alive.

Love and thanks to my incredible community of friends and family—especially Claudia, Joshua, Christian, Wilson, Steph, Mom, Dad, Nick, Miguel, Dejlig, Mogens, and Morten—for their support, patience, and encouragement. Apologies to Trey for the Britpop blasphemy.

Finally, thank you to Leah Babb-Rosenfeld, Benedict O'Hagan, and all the folks at Bloomsbury for the repeated privilege of seeing my words in print.

Notes

Chapter 2

1 "Albums of the Year." *Melody Maker*, December 24/31, 1988.

Chapter 3

1 Roberts, Chris. "Japanese Whispers." *Melody Maker*, March 18, 1989.

2 Clay, Joe. "Lifting off the Ground: Andy Bell recalls Ride's take-off." *Crypt* [zine], 2019.

Chapter 6

1 Williams, Simon. "De-Lush-Us." *New Musical Express*, October 14, 1989.

2 Simpson, Dave. "Saint Errant." *Melody Maker*, December 9, 1989.

3 Roberts, Chris. "Ride." *Melody Maker*, January 20, 1990.

4 Williams, Simon. "Beyond the Pale." *New Musical Express*, February 10, 1990.

5 Sutherland, Steve. "Lush Lust for Life." *Melody Maker*, February 17, 1990.

6 "Symphonic Chaos." *Melody Maker*, December 1990.

7   Roberts, Chris. "My Bloody Valentine: Glide on Time." *Melody Maker*, April 28, 1990.

8   Price, Simon. *Melody Maker*, August 11, 1990.

9   Williams, Simon. "Hüsker Düing it for the Kids." *New Musical Express*, July 7, 1990.

10 Unsworth, Cathi. "Chapterhouse: Grooves in the House." *Sounds*, September 15, 1990.

11 Morton, Roger. "AAAARGHBIBBLEWIBBLE!" *New Musical Express*, October 20, 1990.

12 "The 50 Best Shoegaze Albums of All Time." *Pitchfork*, October 24, 2016.

13 Williams, Simon. "Ride: Nowhere" [review]. *New Musical Express*.

14 Roberts, Chris. "Ride: Nowhere" [review]. *Melody Maker*, October 6, 1990.

15 "Sweetness and Light." *Melody Maker*, December 22, 1990.

16 Lester, Paul. "Chrome Sweet Chrome." *Melody Maker*, December 1, 1990.

17 "1990 Festive Fifty." *John Peel Wiki*. https://peel.fandom.com/wiki/1990_Festive_Fifty.

18 "Melody Maker End of Year Critic Lists—1990." https://www.rocklistmusic.co.uk/mmlists_p2.htm.

Chapter 8

1   *Melody Maker*, January 5, 1991.

2   Savage, Jon. "Feedback to the Future: My Bloody Valentine." *20/20*, Spring 1991.

3   Stanley, Bob. "Slowdive: Younger Than Yesterday." *Melody Maker*, March 2, 1991.

4   Smith, Matt. "Moose: Horns of Plenty." *Melody Maker*, March 23, 1991.

5   Brown, James. "Singles" [review]. *New Musical Express*, March 23, 1991.

6   Stud Brothers, The. *Melody Maker*, March 9, 1991.

7   Brown, James. "Singles" [review]. *New Musical Express*, March 23, 1991.

8   Sutherland, Steve. "Crash of the Titans." *Melody Maker*, August 10, 1991.

9   Williams, Simon. "Slowdive: Just for a Day." *New Musical Express*, August 24, 1991.

10   Lester, Paul. "Dive Bomb." *Melody Maker*, August 31, 1991.

11   Sutherland, Steve. "Hell on Wheels." *Melody Maker*, September 1991.

12   "Bum Lush to go!" *New Musical Express*, October 19, 1991.

13   Reynolds, Simon. "My Bloody Valentine: Loveless" [review]. *Melody Maker*, November 2, 1991.

14   Fadele, Dele. "My Bloody Valentine: Loveless" [review]. *New Musical Express*, November 9, 1991.

15   Reynolds, Simon. "'Dream-Pop' Bands Define the Times in Britain." *The New York Times*, December 1, 1991.

Chapter 9

1   Ross, Andy. "Shoegazing—The Coining of a Genre." *The Huffington Post*, May 11, 2016.

2 Lamacq, Steve. "Slowdive" [news bulletin]. *New Musical Express*, May 25, 1991.

3 Sutherland, Steve. "Moose: Camden Underworld" [live review]. *Melody Maker*, June 8, 1991.

Chapter 10

1 Quantick, David. "Memoirs of a Shoegazing Gentleman." *New Musical Express*, October 26, 1991.

2 Page, Betty. "Lush: Spooky" [review]. *New Musical Express*, January 18, 1992.

3 Cameron, Keith. "The Boo Radleys: Everything's Alright Forever" [review]. *New Musical Express*, March 21, 1992.

4 Stubbs, David. "Curve: The Bend of the World as We Know It." *Melody Maker*, March 14, 1992.

5 Maconie, Stuart. "Blur: Blast of the Famous International Game Boys." *New Musical Express*, March 28, 1991.

6 "The Best New Band in Britain." *Melody Maker*, April 25, 1992.

7 Williams, Simon. "Drop Nineteens: New York Danceteria" [demo review]. *New Musical Express*, October 5, 1991.

8 True, Everett. "19 Forever." *Melody Maker*, August 1, 1992.

9 Cardew, Ben. "The 50 Best Shoegaze Albums of All Time." *Pitchfork*, October 24, 2016.

10 Lester, Paul. "Whatever Happened to Shoegazing?" *Melody Maker*, September 12, 1992.

Chapter 11

1   "Yanks Go Home!" *Select*, April 1993.

2   Tangari, Joe. "Raise/Mezcal Head" [reissue review]. *Pitchfork*, April 2, 2009.

3   Kulkarni, Neil. "Eight-Legged Snooze Machine" [album review]. *Melody Maker*, March 9, 1996.

Chapter 12

1   Ott, Chris. "Ulrich Schnauss: A Strangely Isolated Place" [review]. *Pitchfork*, June 3, 2003.

2   LeMay, Matt. "M83: Dead Cities, Red Seas & Lost Ghosts" [review]. *Pitchfork*, May 12, 2003.

3   Richardson, Mark. "Top 100 Albums of the 1990s." *Pitchfork*, November 17, 2003.

4   Toner, Paul. "Gen Z Are Resurrecting Shoegaze for Their 'Bleak, Post-COVID World.'" *Vice*, April 27, 2021.

5   Enis, Eli. "TikTok Has Made Shoegaze Bigger Than Ever." *Stereogum*, December 18, 2023.

6   Sherburne, Philip. "The Shoegaze Revival Hit Its Stride in 2023." *Pitchfork*, December 14, 2023.

7   Hall, Michael James. "Drop Nineteens: Hard Light" [review]. *Under the Radar*, November 3, 2023.